"*Barry Moltz has a special combination of wit* *that comes only to those who have pursued their o* *In How to Get Unstuck: 25 Ways to Get Your B* offers a common sense approach and the practical steps any small business can take to address obstacles and get back on the road to success.*"
- Cindy Bates, Vice President of Small Business, Microsoft

"*Stuck but getting by might be the worst trap of all - Moltz unpacks all the reasons you're lodged where you are and shows you how to get back to doing what you love.*"
- John Jantsch,
author of Duct Tape Marketing and Duct Tape Selling

Are you getting in your own way, blocking your path to small business success? In this easy-to-read book, Barry Moltz points out 25 bad habits and negative attitudes keeping small business owners stuck – not achieving greater financial and personal well-being. Moltz provides clear-eyed insights and case studies, sure to help small business owners get over these psychological and operational barriers and finally get unstuck.
- Rhonda Abrams,
author of Successful Business Plan: Secrets & Strategies, Six-Week Start-Up, and USA Today Small Business Columnist

"*The only direction for your business is forward. Barry's book will give you a blueprint for getting unstuck, powering through complexity and adversity and reaching your goals. This easy to act on book will change the way you think about business and life. Buy a copy for yourself or if you manage others, for your whole team.*"
-Tim Sanders,
author of Love Is the Killer App: How To Win Business and Influence Friends

"*Barry Moltz has a habit of writing books you need to think about and execute around, but that you shy away from digging into. Don't make that mistake with this book. Get unstuck already, damn it. The world needs you.*"
- Chris Brogan, publisher Owner Magazine

"Barry Moltz is one of the top go-to people if you're looking for helping running and growing your business. And once again he doesn't disappoint. With "How to Get Unstuck: 25 Ways to Get Your Business Growing Again" Barry provides unique and critical advice for any businessperson, from startup to established owner who needs to "get unstuck."
- Gene Marks CPA, New York Times Blogger

"We all get stuck at one time or another. That is not the question. The question is — what are you going to do about it? The answer is to read Barry's book. I found "How to Get Unstuck" to be chock-full of valuable insights, and useful, actionable tips. An excellent resource."
- Steve Strauss,
Senior USA TODAY Business columnist and author of
The Small Business Bible

"Nobody knows small businesses better than Barry Moltz, and How to Get Unstuck comes along just as I was tempted to allow my own business to sink into a rut. We can always count on Barry to tell us exactly what we need to do - and stop doing - to sustain the momentum so critical for long-term, successful entrepreneurship."
-Alexandra Levit,
author of Blind Spots: The 10 Business Myths You Can't Afford to
Believe on Your New Path to Success

"Read Unstuck and never be short of customers again! I benefited from this book and I know you will too."
- Michael Port, NY Times Bestselling Author
of Book Yourself Solid Illustrated

"Small business success isn't about big wins. It's about being able to keep going when you feel like you're stuck. Barry's book gives you the edge to keep going when other people would give up."
- Penelope Trunk, career coach, author and blogger

"The question isn't if your business will get stuck, the question is when. And when that moment arrives, this book will get you out. Get unstuck now!"
- Mike Michalowicz, Author of The Pumpkin Plan

"For years, Barry Moltz has told small business owners like it is. His advice is solid, through-and-through. With "Get Unstuck," he's at it again. Learn how to work on the business, instead of in it, how to take time off and recharge so you can truly think, how to use social media effectively, and how to say no to the yes men in your organization. When you finish reading this book, you'll truly be unstuck and ready to rule the world."

- Gini Dietrich, CEO Arment Dietrich and author, Spin Sucks

"Great books, brilliant films and genius business ideas are born and die in our minds when we can't figure out how to get unstuck. Of all the people I know, Barry is the master at getting great work done quickly, efficiently and consistently. Heed his advice, and watch your business soar."

-Pamela Slim, bestselling author of Body of Work

How to Get

UNSTUCK

25 Ways to Get Your Business Growing Again

By Barry J. Moltz

Published by Motivational Press, Inc.
7777 N Wickham Rd, # 12-247
Melbourne, FL 32940
www.MotivationalPress.com

Manufactured in the United States of America.

ISBN: 978-1-62865-075-4

CONTENTS

"The only way out is through." —Robert Frost

For small business owners who are stuck, but find a way through.

ACKNOWLEDGEMENTS

This book would never have happened without the guidance of Elizabeth Marshall. She worked with me to develop an outline that was compelling and fun to write. Thank you, Liz.

Ethan, Daniel, and Sara, the centers of my life, who always patiently listen to my crazy anecdotes one more time.

Sei Shihan Nancy Lanoue and Jun Shihan Sarah Ludden, my Seido karate teachers at Thousand Waves, who teach me what to do when things get tough, how to face them head on and come through the other side. A deep bow of appreciation!

My parents, Alan and Carole, who have always encouraged me to pursue my passion.

Mike Cooper, an inspiring businessperson and my step father-in-law, may he rest in peace, who always found a way to get unstuck and move forward.

Senpai Sam Boyer, who did a lot of research for this book. If colleges are producing young writers like Sam, we are getting our money's worth.

Marla Markman, who patiently edited this book and made me sound like I knew what I was talking about. Her advice was invaluable.

Rieva Lesonsky, for being my mentor and for writing the foreword for this book. You inspire me.

FOREWORD

Stop Struggling, Help is On the Way

Being a small business owner is like living the opening sentence in the Charles Dickens' classic *A Tale of Two Cities*, "It was the best of times, it was the worst of times, it was the age of wisdom, it was the age of foolishness, it was the epoch of belief, it was the epoch of incredulity, it was the season of Light, it was the season of Darkness, it was the spring of hope, it was the winter of despair, we had everything before us, we had nothing before us . . ."

Sound familiar? When we start out, we're filled with hope, positivity and optimism. We experience those amazing days when it seems nothing can stop us as we move ahead.

And then comes, as Dickens writes, "the season of Darkness," where even the smallest hurdle looms like Mt. Everest. And in an instant, we're stuck. It's like treading water—we work and work and work and yet we never move ahead.

Nothing is more frustrating. Especially since getting stuck often takes small business owners by surprise. We're not aware of what we did to get in this situation, and we have no idea how to get out. Yet, with every passing day we know, if we don't get unstuck, we're going to go under—and lose our businesses.

But how—how do we do that? How *do* we get unstuck? The life of a small business owner can be a lonely and isolating one. So often we don't have anyone to tell us the truth, to show us what we did wrong, how to make it right and make sure we don't make the same mistake again. In short, we don't have—but we do need our own Jiminy Cricket.

You all remember Jiminy—he tried to keep Pinocchio out of trouble, rescued him when misfortune befell him anyway, and helped him realize his dream of becoming a real boy. Unfortunately, most of us don't have a singing cricket to save us. But we do have Barry Moltz.

Think of Barry as your own Jiminy Cricket. In fact he wrote this book, *How to Get Your Business Unstuck*, to help you the same way Jiminy aided Pinocchio. From the moment I first met Barry, he told me his mission was to help small business owners get unstuck and move forward once again.

Barry believes there are 25 all too common ways small business owners get themselves in a morass. In this book he not only identifies the problems, he offers the solutions, accompanied by real-life case studies of companies just like yours that once were stuck and broke free.

Every small business owner will recognize himself or herself in these pages. Are you afraid to turn down business? Do you have a social media strategy? Do you (or your employees) secretly hate your customers? Do you think it's a sign of weakness to admit you need help? A "yes" answer to any of those questions could indicate you're stuck.

Don't worry, help is on the way. You can get unstuck. You already took the first step by buying this book. Turn the page and let Barry Moltz help you. As Jiminy once said, "You can't shoulder all by your problems alone, ya know."

Rieva Lesonsky
CEO/Co-founder
GrowBiz Media
SmallBizDaily.com

INTRODUCTION

You would not exactly call your business a smashing success, but you have made enough money over the years to keep your company going. You have always weathered the ups and downs, but recently, it has become more difficult to grow a profitable business. Every month, you are in the habit of searching to find new customers and revenue to keep your business going. You are constantly worried about cash flow and replacing the employees who always seem to quit or get fired. The company is not growing the way you thought it would when you started.

You wake every morning feeling like you are on a never-ending hamster wheel. You have tried many things to turn it around, but you have failed. As a result, both your energy and interest are waning. You and your business are literally stuck. After running your company for many years, it has sapped your energy and life out of you. You keep looking for that magic bullet that will be "the tipping point" to take it to the next level. You hope the next big customer or new employee will make the difference. Unfortunately, that brave knight on a white horse never seems to come.

You are at the point where you aren't going out of business, but you're not getting rich either. While this scraping by gives you a job, you are not building a sustainable business. The worst part is that you see few opportunities to grow the company or a way to earn a living elsewhere.

Do any of these situations sound familiar? You are not alone, and help is right inside this book. Many small business owners have felt the same way as you do. They have not been able to get unstuck and start growing again. But "the tipping point" is as easy as recognizing what is holding your business back and what changes need to be made to turn it around.

This book reveals the 25 most common reasons why companies get stuck and how to fix them. Case studies also illustrate success stories. There is no need to read this book sequentially. There may even be some repetition in the topics because small business owners tend to approach the same problems from slightly different angles. Pick the topic or particular symptom that most closely matches what you and your company are going through right now. That is always the best place to start.

1. You Treat Your Business like it's a Job

You are so desperate to earn enough money to support your family this month that you don't make any future investments that would result in building a stronger business. As a result, you say yes too quickly to what customers want you to do for them. Your business has drifted from your original focused mission, and you are not sure where it is headed.

2. You Think that Your Latest Successful Windfall Will Last Forever

Once financial success comes, you think you have found the magic formula and you have the "Midas Touch." You feel you will never fail again, and you start to believe your own press. You begin to surround yourself with "yes" people who tell you how great you are no matter what happens.

3. You Think Someone is Coming to Save You

You are desperate for that magic bullet. You keep thinking the next employee or big customer will turn around your business. You keep looking for the white knight to ride into town to make everything OK.

4. You Let Today's "Emergencies" Dictate Your Plan

You start your day by checking Facebook, LinkedIn, and Twitter. Your daily plan falls apart 15 minutes after arriving at the office. You are addicted to multitasking and constantly let yourself be interrupted by people and electronic notifications. You think that by juggling multiple balls in the air, you will be more productive.

5. You Never Take a Break or a Vacation from Work

You have a fear of falling behind or missing an opportunity. You let technology invade every part of your life. You measure success by being busy, not productive.

6. You Take Dangerous Risks Instead of Calculated Actions

You think success is about taking gigantic risks, so you waste your resources by jumping in without first testing the water. You take courses of action that satisfy your ego but don't help your business.

7. You Think the Only Alternative to Success Is Failure

You are afraid of being a failure, so you don't know when to quit or admit it's over. You stop taking risks. And as a result, you keep going, despite increasingly low chances of success.

8. Your Customers Can't Find You

You are marketing where customers can't find you when they are looking to buy. Your business never gets into the "maybe pile" and, therefore, never has a chance of being chosen.

9. Your Fear of Rejection Stops You from Selling

You are afraid of the word "no." You think that when they reject your product or service, they are rejecting you personally. This prevents you from spending the necessary time doing sales and marketing.

10. You Keep Calling People Who Don't Respond

You keep calling or emailing big customer opportunities that never reply. You hold onto the idea that they may still be interested if you bug them enough. This prevents you from talking to other prospects that may be interested.

11. You Stop Marketing as Soon as Your Revenue Increases

That is, you only market when you have no revenue, but as soon as you get customers again, you stop marketing. This keeps the sales in your business flat.

12. You Are Always Selling Product Features

Your product is superior in every way to the competition, yet you only tout your product's features instead of its benefits. With the Internet, prospects can research your features on their own. You are not giving them what they really want—value.

13. You Are Selling a Product that can be Purchased Cheaper Elsewhere

You think your product is unique and that if you build it, people will come because of how incredible it is. Unfortunately, your product has become a commodity without any real value, so customers buy it cheaper elsewhere. You cut your prices, but it is becoming difficult to stay profitable.

14. You Go On Social Media Sites Without a Strategy

You think you don't need a strategy, and besides, surfing social media is a lot of fun! You become more interested in gossip than helping business prospects. You think the sole purpose of social media is to sell your products.

15. You Hate Your Customers (and Maybe Even Your Employees or Vendors)

It's hard to admit, but you really hate your customers. You think they are whiners and are always impossible to please. Come to think of it, this is exactly the way you feel about your employees and vendors.

16. You Only Hire Employees Who Are Weaker Than You

You are afraid of people knowing more than you or making you look bad to your peers, vendors, or customers. As an "A" Player, you only hire "B or C" players in supporting roles. You continue to use a hub-and-spoke organization where all important decisions come through you.

17. You Allow Lousy Employees (and Customers) to Overstay Their Welcome

You don't fire employees, even though everyone knows they are doing a bad job and hurting the company. You can't admit you made a mistake, for fear of the repercussions if you actually let them go.

18. You Hire for Skills, not Attitude

You are in a rush to hire anyone to fill a job. You only ask questions about skills and past experience in the interview process. You never discuss their career goals or how they fit into the company.

19. You Are Always Telling Employees What to Do Because You're the Boss

You think being the boss means ordering people around and threatening them if it does not get done. This is the way it was done at your last company, and it seemed to work well enough.

20. You Think Customer Service Is a Cost Center

You are so busy bringing customers in the front door; you leave the back door wide open for them to leave. You spend all your resources on attracting new customers and don't focus on keeping the ones you have.

21. You Never Ask for Help

You believe that asking for help is a sign of weakness. You think that small business ownership is a solo sport. You are the biggest "I" in "team."

22. You Allow Personal Use of Smartphones on the Job

You do not have any rules in place, and you do not monitor their usage. You can't help think that this activity keeps them distracted from effectively doing their jobs.

23. You Don't Know How to Read Your Financial Statements

You never review them or ask for help to understand what they mean for your business. You believe the numbers that are in your head, rather than the ones on paper. As a result, you make all business decisions blindly. This leads you to borrowing and spending money based on expected results, which gets you into debt.

24. You Think Business Is About Growing Sales

You are so focused on growth and the sales top line (and want to brag about it), that you forget all the other financial measurements. As a result, you never seem to have enough cash to run your company.

25. Your Fixed Overhead Costs Are Too High

Either you didn't forecast your sales and expenses correctly, or you let your ego control the checkbook. You don't know the difference between fixed and variable costs.

CHAPTER 1

You Treat Your Business like It's a Job

WHY YOU ARE STUCK

You started your own business for many reasons. You were tired of working for someone else, and that perennial nine to five had become a real drag. Or maybe you just hated your boss. Maybe you were one of those entrepreneurs who had a burning idea they knew exactly what customers really wanted. Maybe you wanted to set a good example for your family and be able to support them doing something you were passionate about. Besides, your last job had become a grind with limited financial potential, and you were sure you needed more money for the future. Does this sound familiar?

Strangely, after several years, having your own business is starting to feel just like that job. You're working all the time and worrying even more. Some days, as you stare at the mounting bills, you have yet to see that "unlimited financial potential". You are so desperate to meet your financial obligations (the company's and your family's) that you operate the business with a very short-term view, using only immediate tactics to get to any scrap of success.

Your Actions Are Reflected in All Phases of the Business

With customers: In an effort to extract every sales dollar for your business, your company has become all things to all people. You say "yes" too quickly to every request from anyone who even closely resembles a paying customer. For example, you started out in a retail business selling lawnmowers but ended up as a service-based company when you said yes to customers who were asking you to fix their mowers, mow their lawns, or do their landscaping. While many successful businesses need to "pivot" or "morph," potential customers are making all the decisions for you. You have become reactive instead of proactive. You are thinking so short-term that you only charge based on time, not the value customers are receiving for solving their problems. As a result, your business has drifted from its original mission and any type of long-term success.

With money: You think your monthly cash flow is negative since you are always out of money. But you are unsure and you don't know by how much because you never look at a cash flow statement (in fact, you never learned to read one). As a result, you are forced to borrow money to pay for past losses or vendor obligations. Your business feels upside down since current receivables are paying past payables not associated with generating that revenue.

With staff: You are so eager to fill a position (or not wanting to do a job yourself) that you hire anyone who is available. This includes people who not only don't have the proven skills for the job but applicants whose attitudes don't fit into the company culture. In addition, you aren't willing to pay to hire a person who can excel at the job long-term but instead only want "butts in seats." You believe that you can train anyone to do the job, but you don't have a process or the time to make it happen. You also include an "I" in team. As the owner, you *are* the business since you do all the important jobs. Your organization chart looks like hub (you) and spoke (everyone else). If you are busy or away from the business, it ceases to operate profitably. In fact, if you get hit by a bus, the business has no future value.

With vendors: You continue to negotiate the prices on each individual product you sell instead establishing long-term relationships with a handful of key vendors. You view all vendors as adversaries to the success of your business instead of as partners. You don't have time to visit them personally and don't take an interest in their company's goals.

With family: You always pay yourself last. In fact, when doing the budget or looking at the profit and loss statement, there isn't even a line item for owner compensation. You think that as long as you keep the company afloat, you will figure out how to pay your personal bills later. You are always making excuses to your spouse as to why you can't take more money out of the business. Your family laments that at least when you worked for a company, the paycheck was steady and you were home more. Now, you always have to work nights and sacrifice important family events to complete business tasks. In reality, when you are at home, your mind is still at your company.

You have stopped making long-term investments that might build a stronger business due to an increasing doubt that there might not be a company in the future. You operate from a place of fear, not confidence. To many people, you seem desperate. The fear of not meeting payroll and personal bills rules your daily decision-making. You are wondering what went so wrong.

HOW TO GET UNSTUCK

Follow these steps to start building a business and not just a job:

1. **Articulate again the long-term vision.** Reread your first business plan to understand why the business was started initially. What was the spark and passion that launched it? Ask key managers, customers, and advisors their point of view. Get both internal and external perspectives on this vision and how the company has evolved over time. While strategies and tactics might change, core values and company purpose usually stay constant.

2. **What pain does your company alleviate?** In any economy, people buy more painkillers than vitamins. What pain does the business kill

for potential customers? It is critical to know the pain and its solution before targeting a particular customer segment. Think in terms of pain, not needs or wants, since those may not be enough for a customer to take action to buy a product or switch to using your company.

3. **Who is your customer?** Without money coming in, you are running a charity. Most small businesses don't intentionally run a nonprofit. But if you don't know who your customer is and how they will find you once they are ready to buy, then that will be the outcome. The profile of this targeted customer should be very detailed. In addition to ensuring they have the pain your company can solve, note whether they are male or female. What are their ages, income levels, and demographics? Where do they currently shop or talk about their pain (online or offline)?

4. **What are your annual financial goals?** Your goals should not only cover profit for the company but take-home pay for you as the owner. Your compensation should include a reasonable return on investment for your time and money. Company revenue doesn't matter, but rather profit and cash flow. Successful service companies can make 20% profit before taxes. For manufacturers, profit depends on the gross margin level, but these can be as high as 30%. To achieve your financial goals requires disciplined semiannual budgeting and reading the company's financial statements monthly. Always jealously guard your profit and don't always reinvest it in growing the business.

5. **What are the critical success factors, resources, and investments that will be needed to achieve your financial goals?** This plan should be as detailed as possible. For example, what are three critical steps that must happen to attain your goal? One may be to hire an experienced operations manager. Another could be to acquire a large brand as a customer, which can be used as a reference. How much money needs to be

invested in infrastructure and people to achieve your goal? This is best determined by doing a systems and skills inventory. List which people skills the company needs when it has achieved its goals. Then make a checkmark next to each skill the organization has and how likely that person is to stay with the company for the next few years. A similar inventory should be done for infrastructure. How large can the company get with the current infrastructure and can additional functionality be added? Determine what is absolutely necessary to support the revenue goal. Think bigger so systems and processes don't need to be replaced every year. How much can be supported by off-the-shelf products or cloud-based solutions to keep the initial investment low?

6. **How does the business make money?** It is critical to understand all the factors that go into the basic revenue model:

- **Number of customers:** Does the business need a few large ones or purchases from many smaller ones? Do the infrastructure, organization, and people skills support this type of customer base?

- **Revenue per customer:** What is the mean amount of revenue a customer brings in per year? Average revenue can be misleading, especially if there are a few large customers.

- **Cost of goods/service:** What are the direct costs to provide the product or service? How does that cost go up or down based on volume? This will determine the all-important gross margin, which has a big influence on net profit.

- **Customer acquisition:** What does it cost to acquire a customer, and what is their average lifetime value? How are customers acquired? What are the most effective methods? Referrals and online reputation reviews should be a big part of any acquisition strategy.

- **Product development:** What does it cost for the initial product development? Large up-front development costs present a higher risk but can be more profitable long-term if the product is successful. Once the product is introduced, what are its ongoing product improvements or customer service costs?

7. **Where are the key leverage points in your company?** Are your profitable economies of scale based on people, product, intellectual property, proprietary distribution agreements, or customer annuities?

- **People:** In service businesses, the more people who are hired, the more profit that can be made if fixed costs remain constant. Typical gross margins are 50%. This should include all people costs, such as salary, taxes, and benefits. *Example: consulting or other service-oriented businesses*

- **Product:** Once a product is developed, are the variable costs relatively low in producing each additional unit? *Example: computer software and video games where each individually downloaded purchase has very little cost*

- **Intellectual property:** While this is frequently touted as a sustainable competitive advantage with a high barrier to entry, it is difficult to protect, especially when a well-funded competitor tries marketing a duplicate product. Find a good lawyer and don't depend on this to keep the company growing. *Example: software companies*

- **Proprietary distribution agreements:** Locking up long-term exclusive distribution agreements can be profitable but difficult to maintain. *Example: Ace Hardware and SP Richards Office Supply*

- **Customer annuities:** Business with high switching costs and barriers to exit can very be profitable. *Example: cable TV, medical devices, and accounting software*

8. **Who are your best customers?** Size doesn't matter. You just want to know which customers are the most profitable (use the formula: gross

sales-returns-cost of goods or service). Calculating this number will be a surprise since many times the biggest (and most demanding) customers are the least profitable. Also realize that some customers can add more to the bottom line than revenue. For example, do they refer other customers? Have they been with the company a long time? Are they a well-known and trusted brand? Do they give honest company feedback on their products and performance?

When all of this information is known, it will be easier to decide which investments will yield the strongest cash flow and growth for the business.

CASE STUDY
THE POWER OF MANY
MOTIVQUEST

Ten years ago, David Rabjohns started MotiveQuest. He envisioned a next-generation market research consultancy and pioneered a new approach—"online anthropology". His company built a tool that could use organic online conversations to research why people behave the way they do, and how companies could address it. Rabjohns findings interested Fortune 500 companies right away.

At the beginning, this meant that he had to find the customers, run the software, and produce the reports all by himself. He realized that his first hire needed to be a technology guy to help scale the solution. He hired Brook Miller, a brilliant technologist from Intel as his CTO. As the company continued to grow and Rabjohns hired strategists to assist him, he still had to be the lead on every single project. This was limiting the company's growth and burning him out. Rabjohns decided that his second major hire would be Kirsten Recknagel as his COO. She had most recently been the Research Director at Gartner. Recknagel was able to direct the client services team, while Rabjohns focused on sales. When he felt comfortable with her leading that unit, he then hired a Vice President of Sales, Zackery Nippert, previously head of business development at DDB. This enabled Rabjohns to get out of the day-to-day managing of the company and focus on longer term strategy and relationships.

CHAPTER 2

You Think Your Latest Successful Windfall Will Last Forever

WHY YOU ARE STUCK

Welcome King Midas. For most small business owners, financial success is an uphill battle over a long period of time. Many sacrifices are made, much money is spent, and there is little time to spend with family and friends. So once success finally arrives, you begin to believe that you have finally found the magic formula. The door now appears to be wide open for all your business dreams. Jokingly, you even think about having people call you "King Midas" because you believe that everything you touch will turn to gold. Now that you are over the hump, you think you can't ever fail again. Your fancy office, new car, and designer clothes are all a reflection of your new attitude. The mounting accolades from your friends, peers, and social media are poured on to celebrate your success. You start to believe all the wonderful things people are saying. Most important, you now have the financial resources to surround yourself with "yes" people who tell you how great you are, no matter what happens inside your business. You are relieved that they have stopped questioning you and are supportive of every decision you make.

Success does not always beget success. This financial windfall may be more money than you have ever seen or hoped to make. You start to spend freely and somewhat recklessly. You justify it by saying it's a release for all those pent up years of frugality. Spouses, children, relatives, and friends start to ask you to buy them things. You aren't worried since you honestly believe that this success automatically brings more success. You remember that Mia Hamm, a very talented professional soccer player says, "Success breeds success." In some ways, you think you are now entitled to more success.

One success does not a chain make. Based on your success, you begin to expand your business. You believe you can use the same formula that made you successful in one location (or industry area) to achieve success in another—and another. Clearly, customers in a new market will be impressed by the success you have achieved in another part of the country, world, or separate industry. You thought that your brand reputation would carry these customers right to your front door.

HOW TO GET UNSTUCK

Don't look to the past. Past success is never a guarantee for the future. Look at any stock price of a publically traded company. Think Blockbuster Video and Borders. Talk to any successful entrepreneur. Overnight success takes seven to ten years, and even then, there are no guarantees. Just think about where the windfalls of most lottery winners have gone. And don't forget all those one-hit musical wonders, like The Ides of March ("Vehicle") and Tommy Tutone ("867-5309/Jenny"). According to Mary-Lynn Foster and George Krueger, owners of consulting firm BIGG Success, success can breed affirmations, confidence, enthusiasm, and energy, but it also can breed failure. Many people get overconfident and take too much risk. They stop doing what they did in the first place to get them to where they are. Instead, they look for shortcuts and try to convince themselves that they will be successful solely based on their past success. No business is immune. Even major successful companies have a long list of failures. Think Ben-Gay Aspirin, Virgin Cola, Apple's Newton, Cosmopolitan Yogurt, Life Savers Soda, Coors Water, Colgate Kitchen

Entrees, Frito-Lay Lemonade, Bic underwear, Harley Davidson Perfume, and Sony's Betamax.

The phenomenon of success not bringing more success has been statistically documented in basketball. A 1985 study, *The Hot Hand in Basketball: On the Misperception of Random Sequences*, states, "The chances of success on the next shot are not correlated with the success of the last shot. In other words, the 'hot hand' idea is a fallacy." To increase your chances of success in the future, look to see what conditions exist in the market to make the company successful now, not in the past. Evaluate past results, but do not base future actions solely on them. Don't say, "Well, it worked in the past, so it should work in the future!" Don't make cause-and-effect connections where they do not exist. Keep thinking like a start-up entrepreneur as long as possible. This worked for IBM in the late '70s and early '80s. The company moved the work on the new personal computer they were developing to a separate business unit so the effort would not be "weighed down" by IBM's past success in unrelated areas.

Don't over expand. Bigger is not always better. Don't over expand. Companies that have recently franchised tend to make this mistake. They either send their best talent to the new location (and the existing one falls apart), or they send a new person who does not know the company's business well enough to make the new location successful. Before expanding, make sure you have the capital, infrastructure, and people to achieve success. Expect that the performance of your existing operations will suffer for the first year after opening a new retail location or office.

Plan for zero. Most businesses experience ups and downs. As a result, every business needs to "plan for zero." I wrote about this in my book *Small Town Rules*. My coauthor, Becky McCray, and I stated:

"Every business will experience ups and downs. Just like farmers prepare for years when they will have a crop failure, smart entrepreneurs everywhere prepare for down years and lean months. When smart entrepreneurs have a

big score or a super year, they put some money in savings. They prepare for those down years. One way entrepreneurs do that is with a long-term plan, perhaps five years or longer. Five years is a long time, as advances are made every day. Looking multiple years down the road forces smart entrepreneurs to face the fact that decisions today have long-term effects. Always save enough money in the business for when more difficult times inevitably hit in the economic cycle."

Be frugal again. Practice the same budgeting techniques you did to get to this successful place. In many cases, too much money can make business owners stupid. They start to throw money at the problem instead of using their brainpower to find a solution. Like a start-up, bootstrap and test with cheap solutions before more expensive investments are made. Small tests will eventually lead to big profits because they allow the company to adjust and change directions, which provides the best chance for success.

Develop independent, thinking managers. Every small business owner needs to build a management team, outside advisory board, and stable of employees that complement their skills. This can prove difficult, because on some level, owners do not want to be questioned. They want everyone to love what they do. But you need to create an environment where all employees are encouraged to give honest feedback. There should never be a penalty for disagreements in the discussion phase before a decision and course of action is taken. To ensure that you do not overly influence your team, ask managers and employees for feedback *before* you give your own opinion. Remember, you do not always have to take their advice, but all employees need to know that you valued and considered it.

Hire an advisory board. Every small business should eventually have an advisory board. These should be trusted individuals (not customers) who can give you honest feedback without penalty of being fired. They should be hired for at least a year and be paid quarterly for their advice.

They are in the best position to keep the owner humble and give them the outside perspective that many lose inside their own company.

Form a customer council. This is different from an advisory board. Remember these people are still your customers, so you may not want to share all the company's warts. Customer councils can give outside insight for testing of new products and services. "How is your company really doing?" That's what a customer council can determine on an ongoing basis. They can tell you where the company can find customers just like them. An additional advantage is the more vested they are in the success of your company, the more likely they will stay as a customer and refer others. (Chapter 12 discusses why positive reviews from your customer community are one of the most powerful forms of marketing today.)

CASE STUDY

THE RICH DON'T ALWAYS GET RICHER

WHITTMAN-HART

In 1990, I left my nine-year career at IBM to work for a client of mine, Bob Bernard, CEO of Whittman-Hart. I was hired to be director of sales for this national computer consulting business. The company had enjoyed a great deal of success over its first six years and had offices in Chicago and Indianapolis. Bernard directed me to expand the sales team nationally and open offices in Los Angeles and Virginia. Because of the company's success, we felt we could not fail. Company executives (including myself) wore $1,000 Armani and Hugo Boss suits to match Bernard's style. It is the only company I have worked at where the men dressed better than the women. The atmosphere resembled the TV movie, *Billionaire Boys Club*.

What I soon found out was what made the company successful in Chicago did not work in the other locations. Bernard had built a solid reputation over the years in Chicago and had a primary client (Reynolds Metals) that allowed the company to build a big stable of varying technical talent that could be used at other local locations if needed. However, in these new, remote locations, we started with sales reps but provided little technical sales talent. Our reps were so used to being successful that they assumed when they showed up in town in their fancy suits, they would automatically be a hit. The prospects (and competitors) were not impressed. Technical resources were needed at these remote locations, but they could not be spared for multiple days without affecting current clients. When these locations did finally land a client, hiring new technical talent could not be shared across multiple customers to make it profitable. As a result, we had to reset our expectations of how quickly these new, remote locations could be successful and how much profit they would take out of the main Chicago operation. We also had to decide which locations we could invest enough resources in for them to be successful and pull back from those areas where we were unable to make the investment. All this ended up being a costly mistake for the company and me. We closed some of the sales offices after large losses. In addition, as director of sales, I lost my job at the company as a result of this failure. Another lesson learned.

CHAPTER 3

You Think Someone Is Coming to Save You

WHY YOU ARE STUCK

You get desperate to find the magic bullet. When you first started the business, you were patient. People told you that every successful business takes time. You even recall that famous platitude that "good things come to those who wait." Now you think you have waited long enough! You keep believing the next employee or big customer sale will turn around your business and finally take it to that next level. It will be that "tipping point" that Malcolm Gladwell talks so much about. The warning signs that you are looking for a white knight to save you are everywhere:

The next customer: You chase that big contract from a name-brand customer. You make promises you are not sure you can keep and still make a profit. You begin to publicize your success with this customer, even before the results come in. Unfortunately, these large contracts with even bigger expectations almost never work out as initially projected. They usually lead to under-performance and disappointment on both sides because you are so hungry for that next big opportunity that you will promise almost anything to get your foot in the door. But the opposite happens: It gets even harder to find another big opportunity.

The next employee: You can finally hire a very experienced employee or manager from a competitor or large corporation. They promise to bring customers, expertise, and other contacts with them. Score! On the contrary—this is one of the biggest hiring mistakes you can make. It's very difficult for a high-level executive to go from working at a large established enterprise to leading a small entrepreneurial venture. Many times the executive turns out to be a corporate manager instead of an entrepreneurial leader. The worst part is you paid this person a lot of money and they were gone within a year. This happened in 1990, when I left being a marketing manager at IBM to become the director of sales for a small computer services company. I soon realized I was ill equipped to lead my team. At IBM, I had a large support infrastructure and a long established brand culture to lean on. At the new company, none of my training helped me run a small national sales organization. As a result, I was fired a year later (as discussed in the case study in Chapter 2).

The next product line: This is the product or service you have been waiting to roll out to customers for years. In fact, you believe that it is exactly what your customers have been asking for. You have invested so much into the development of this product that it just "has to work." Again, miscalculations and other sky-high expectations sink the results. You are left with few resources to launch another large product.

The next consultant: He has written books and has a long list of experience. His past clients always sing his praises. He has convinced you that he knows the answer to all your problems. His solutions may even have fancy names. To you, he can do no wrong and he will deliver the answers that will turn your company around. This does not happen, however, since one person cannot fix it all in a short period of time, especially someone on the outside. You fire the consultant and begin your search for a new one who will really make it happen this time.

The next market change: You keep saying you have been ahead of the market curve for a long time. You have been waiting years for the market to finally catch up to your brilliance. You reason that it is now your company's time to shine. Unfortunately, the market seems to be leapfrogging past your company or pivots in an unforeseen direction. You are left wondering how this happened.

The next competitor: This was your archrival and business nemesis. They finally went out of business, and your company is the only one left standing. Now customers have no choice but to buy from you. Wrong! A new or complementary solution enters the marketplace and customers instead flock to them.

Unfortunately, none of these white knights saves your business. This only leaves you more distraught, depressed, and somewhat hopeless about the future. According to marketing expert Seth Godin, one of the reasons this happens is because of the lies we tell ourselves in business:

"The first lie is that you're going to need far more talent than you were born with. The second lie is that the people who are leading in the new connection economy got there because they have something you don't. The third lie is that you have to be chosen. The fourth lie is that we're not afraid. We're afraid. Afraid to lead, to make a ruckus, to convene. Afraid to be vulnerable, to be called out, to be seen as a fraud."

HOW TO GET UNSTUCK

Success is built through patient interim steps, not by taking big leaping risks. Popular wisdom seems to suggest that the biggest payouts go to the person who takes the biggest risks. However, when the success story is publicized, no one hears about all the interim steps that were taken to get to the final result. No one sees the up, down, and sideways path it took to reach the goals.

Forget the giant risks. It is much more effective to make a decision, examine its result, and learn what you can. Then make another decision based on that outcome. Think of each small decision as another piece of completing a puzzle. Never pin the future of your company on one decision, action, or resource. Here is what to do with each of the next new, exciting opportunities:

The next customer: Downsize expectations. Start with small sales goals. No matter how big the opportunity or how famous the brand, keep the excitement in check. While you may not want to treat them like just another customer, assume sales will build very slowly over a long period of time. It is rare that your largest customer starts out that way. In many cases, the first-year revenue for any customer is usually half what is expected, and the expenses to support that customer are four times as much. Many successful businesses have at least 10 customers that make up 80% of their business.

The next employee: Be realistic. On any team, a new player can have an impact. But typically this takes some time. Before hiring, find out if the prospective employee truly has demonstrated he or she can do the job. Having previous experience at a competitor or a large brand-name company may not translate to success at your business. Be as objective and critical as possible. Have you tested their skills as part of the hiring process? This can be done just as easily for knowledge workers as for those who perform a physical task. Hiring success is not tied to one employee. It happens by building a team with a strong culture, over a long period of time.

The next product line: Has it really been beta tested? What have the initial customers said about the product? How can it be rolled out to a small release to ensure it works as expected? Have these initial customers paid for the product and what real results have they accrued as a result? Most products take time to be adapted by the marketplace. This also usually happens when supported by a substantial marketing budget. Remember that only 125,000 iPods were sold the first year they were introduced (last year 350 million were sold).[1]

The next consultant: No matter how good their experience, one person cannot make a huge impact immediately. Start the consultant with a small scoped project with stated goals. At the project's completion, match the goal against the actual results. Be critical. If the outcome is positive, do a second project and build scale from there. As discussed later, you should have a series of outside advisors to get a range of viewpoints, rather than depending on one person.

The next market change: Test, test, and test. Do this before a large investment is made in project development or a big marketing expense rollout. Have you really identified a pain in the market from people who can pay to fill it? This is only demonstrated by paying repeat customers (and referrals) and not with what prospects say when you survey them. Many people will say yes when surveyed, but few will say yes when you actually ask them for money.

The next competitor: Competitors always come and go from the market. What a customer substitutes for one product is constantly changing, so it's difficult to keep up. Know everything customers do with the same money they use to buy your products or services. Keep up to date on all these competitors, and track where they are making their largest investments. As Chinese general Sun Tzu said, "Keep your friends close and your enemies closer."

CASE STUDY
LOOKING FOR MY WHITE KNIGHT
SCITECH

I started SciTech with a partner to sell niche software. Before search engines on the Internet, this company sold technical and scientific software through mail order catalogs. This was before there were computer superstores and search engines. In the mid to late '90s, we began e-commerce on the Internet. I always thought we were at the tipping point with every opportunity that came our way. Over a period of six years, we thought that every "next" was what would take the company to the next level. It didn't exactly work out that way.

The next customer: We landed a big government customer that promised to buy a lot of products from us in exchange for deep discounts. They got the price they wanted, but the high volume never materialized because they were restricted on how much product they could buy through new vendors on an annual basis.

The next employee: We were able to hire a top executive from a competitor. Unfortunately, this new employee did not fit into our company culture and did not have the skills we needed. He was at the competitor when they went through a high-growth stage, but I realized too late that he had little to do with driving growth. He was a beneficiary of the company's success, not the reason for it.

The next product line: The company landed a big national product line form a publically traded company. Unfortunately, while the demand was strong, there was very little margin for selling the product. Shipping so much of this product stressed the infrastructure the company had built for high-margin and low-volume orders. This eventually hurt our overall profitability.

The next consultant: She had helped other companies in similar industries. Unfortunately, the consultant's knowledge turned out to be stale and no longer relevant as the market shifted. She charged too much with very limited results.

The next market change: The company expanded from software to hardware. Customers never made the transition to buying this type of product from us since they were already locked into hardware-sourcing deals. We found out that decisions for large hardware purchases were made by a different set of decision makers than those who bought our specialized high-price software. These products also took up a lot of room in the warehouse and hurt our efficient software-picking process.

The next competitor: Our largest competitor went out of business. But instead of their customers flooding to us, they decided to buy from a series of much smaller niche distributors (or directly from the manufacturers) that were never even on the radar.

CHAPTER 4

You Let Today's "Emergencies" Dictate Your Plan

WHY YOU ARE STUCK

The sky is falling. You approach the new workday with a sense of what you can get done and a solid plan. But then you start immediately by checking your Facebook, Twitter, and LinkedIn feeds to get the latest overnight updates. While this may be interesting and fun, today's plan falls apart fifteen minutes after arriving at the office. Instead of spending five minutes on these sites, you spend thirty. What's worse, they add a new distraction you had not even thought about thirty minutes ago. Unlimited access to the World Wide Web can start to be a worldwide waste of time.

As the day progresses, you start to furiously multitask to make up for the amount of work that now needs to get done. In fact, you become addicted to doing multiple things at one time. In your mind, being busy means that you are productive. As a result, you constantly let yourself be interrupted by people, phone calls, and many other electronic notifications. This seems responsive and completes at least "the small stuff." Social media expert, Chris Brogan, says that we are "addicted to distraction." You go looking for emergencies because it makes you feel more useful and gives the perfect excuse for not focusing on other critical long-term issues that are waiting for you.

You have become an addict. Science shows that social media is physically addictive. This is because using it stimulates the production of a neurotransmitter in the brain called dopamine. Dopamine is the "seeking" or "hunting" chemical; it stimulates curiosity and makes people want to achieve or get something. When you feel stimulated and excited at the prospect of some new challenge or task, you are experiencing a dopamine rush.

Counterbalancing the "seeking" chemical are the "reward" chemicals, the *opioids*. You know that warm, satisfied feeling you get from completing a difficult task? That is opioids telling you that the job is done and you do not need to seek anymore.

When people use social media, they are stimulating both their seeking and reward systems at an extremely quick rate. This is a powerful combination. As soon as people log on to their social media accounts, they are bombarded by dozens of things to do, messages to send and reply to, and "like" buttons to click. Every one of these tasks creates a dopamine rush, and when each one is complete, it's capped off with an opioid reward.

Since social media updates so frequently, there are always new tasks to complete, making any social media account a never-ending supply of dopamine and opioid stimulation. According to Psychology Today, this results in people becoming addicted to their social media accounts. They just can't get enough of those little chemical pick-me-ups, and their work suffers as a result.

You multi- everything. You believe multitasking is a crucial skill and that you are quite good at it. But you are wrong. Multitasking is an inefficient waste of time and energy. Here are three reasons why:

1. **It slows task completion.** Ever notice how your computer seems to grind to a halt when you try to load your word processor, the Internet, a spreadsheet, and then your email all at the same time? When you multitask, you're doing exactly that to your brain. Your brain can only "load" so much at one time, and multitasking can easily overload

it, slowing you down. Your brain can only work on one thing mentally and one thing physically at the same time. The other tasks end up waiting for their turn.

2. **It causes mistakes.** Except for a few super humans, true multitasking is almost impossible. What people really do is called "task switching," where you rapidly shift your attention from one task to the other and back. Rapid task switching can introduce errors by mixing up relevant factors in the job. For example, swapping a digit in a phone number with a crucial numeral in your accounting spreadsheet.

3. **It shortchanges your memory.** It takes a few seconds of concentration and some mental repetition for something in your short-term memory to be stored in your long-term memory. When you multitask, you often do not pay the full amount of attention required to properly process and save memories of your tasks. That's why studying for tests while talking on the phone never worked in school and why talking on the phone while memorizing a presentation doesn't work either.[2]

HOW TO GET UNSTUCK

Stop to think if the emergency is a true emergency. Does it really have to be done now, or does it only seem like an emergency because there is a lot of "noise" around it or because you are looking for an excuse not to do your planned priorities. Determine if someone else can address this emergency. It only needs your attention right now if no one else can handle it and it exceeds in importance the priorities you already have set for today.

Strive for minimal achievement. That's right, minimal achievement. At the end of the previous day, pick two things that are critical to complete the next day so tomorrow is productive, not just busy. Always start with the most critical and unpleasant tasks in the day. It is key to pick two things since the first task may be completed in a shorter period of time than expected or once the task is started, you find that it can't be completed because it is dependent on someone else. If these tasks take more than ninety minutes, they should be broken into smaller pieces. When these two tasks are completed, the day can be declared productive no matter what else happens.

Create to-don't lists. Most to-do lists don't work. People just keep rewriting the same tasks week after week and month after month. The first step in making these lists effective is to cross off everything that does not belong on the list. If it is not an "A" priority today, then it either does not need to be written down or should be delegated to another team member. After identifying the "A" priorities, divide them into tasks, phone calls, and email follow-ups. Work on these grouped tasks together. As Steve Jobs reminded his managers every week, to be innovative and productive, you need to focus on fewer things, not more.

Stop multi-anything. It's tempting to multitask, especially when you have a never-ending amount of work, but dividing your concentration weakens your mind. Bring the full force of your concentration to bear on each task, and you'll not only get them done faster, but you'll also feel less stressed doing them.[3] Turn off your phone and all your email and social media electronic notifications. You decide when to give them attention, not when they beep to get attention from you.

Slow down the flow. When setting a daily plan, think of one of my favorite Zen parables:

There are two monks sitting by a river and talking about the incredible power of their Zen masters. The first monk says, *"My Zen master is so powerful, he can walk across this river without using a bridge."* The second monk says, *"That's nothing. My Zen master is so powerful, that when he chops wood, he chops wood. When he cooks rice, he cooks rice."*

Before asking what this could all mean, go back, and read it again. The second monk says that he can find incredible power by focusing on one thing at a time and doing it extremely well. This has become more difficult as the world is filled with businesspeople that have very short attention spans. Think about the last time you only focused on one thing at a time. Are you reading this book and being interrupted by doing something else? Gotcha!

In the world of instant communication, this is incredibly difficult since most small businesses believe they need to be constantly connected to serve their customers. In reality, things move slower than you think. Different channels of communication require different response rates. For example:

- *Phone:* within 24 hours
- *Text:* within an hour
- *Email:* same business day
- *Blog post comments:* within 4 hours
- *Social media comments:* within 4 hours
- *Mail:* within 24 hours

The most effective strategy is to set communication expectations with a customer up front. The problem is that if you do not set reasonable expectations for them, they will set their own. For example, tell customers phone calls and emails will be returned the same day if made before 3:00 p.m. This can be done via an automated phone message or email auto responder. Staff these communication channels at a pace that can be profitable for the business in the long-term. If you do not have the financial resources to respond in this period of time, do not offer it as a communication channel.

Stop to make a decision and take action. Most decisions are made in an instant, and we spend the rest of the time justifying it before announcing what we will do. Stop fretting. Take enough time to make a calculated decision and take a small action. As discussed in previous chapters, remember that successful companies are not about taking big risks but instead taking a series of patient steps to get to a goal.

Deal with every email once. How many emails do you have in your inbox right now? If it is more than twenty-five, read this section twice. To be productive, it is critical to read every email only once and take action on it. If this is not done, you read the same emails in your inbox over and over to get to the one you really want to take action on. When reading a new email, act on it immediately. In other words, delete, reply, file, or set a follow up. Email rules can be set up so certain messages go directly into a specific folder for action at a later date.

Do not enter a meeting without being prepared. While collaboration is critical in every small business, so much time is wasted in unproductive meetings. For every meeting, plan on the following four items:

1. *An agenda:* What will be discussed and what is the goal of the meeting?

2. *Set time limits:* When will the meeting start and stop? Respect people's time by sticking to this outline.

3. *Not sitting down:* Meetings that are conducted standing up are shorter and just as productive.

4. *An action plan:* Decide what is each participant going to do and by when?

Delegate to others. The only way you can achieve leverage of your time is to delegate. The biggest problem is that many small business owners and managers are horrible at this, and as a result, work longer and harder than most employees.

A famous Harvard management case study, "Who Got the Money?" describes that managers have only a limited amount of time during their day to accomplish tasks. There are three types of time that managers spend: boss-imposed time, used to complete tasks handed down from a superior; system-imposed time, used to complete tasks from peers or from the company bureaucracy; and self-imposed time, used to complete tasks managers create for themselves.

Self-imposed time is divided into two portions. The first is subordinate-imposed time, which is used to complete tasks from subordinates, often to help them solve a problem on the job. The second is discretionary time, which managers can use as they see fit. Subordinate-imposed time takes away from a manager's discretionary time, and overloading on subordinate time can result in constantly being behind on non-urgent (but still important) tasks.

To maximize discretionary time, it is necessary to minimize subordinate-imposed time. When a subordinate comes to a manager with a problem, the natural reaction is for the manager to take the problem onto his or her own shoulders. This causes a role-reversal where the subordinate is waiting on the manager to get something done, which causes the subordinate to do less work while waiting for managerial handholding. In turn, this forces the manager to use valuable discretionary time.

It is important for managers to recognize how they help subordinates with their issues, without taking away the subordinate's initiative. A practical way to do this is to schedule time with subordinates and only address their problems when face-to-face. That way, the manager can make progress on the subordinate's issue, and then give them tasks or suggestions to carry out in their absence. The result will be more discretionary time for the manager, a more organized work life, and more motivated and self-sufficient subordinates.

Live by the code "done is better than perfect." Winners get things done. They are not always done perfectly, but they are able to evaluate their actions and adjust course to reach their goal.

CASE STUDY
OVERCOMING SOCIAL MEDIA ADDICTION
APPLECHEEKS

Ilana Grostern was an ordinary mother of three before she started her online store AppleCheeks, an e-store selling baby products and specializing in diapers. But while the Internet made Ilana into an entrepreneur, it also stuck another label on to her: addict.

Grostern is not addicted to a drug, nor is she a workaholic. She is a self-confessed social media junkie. Ilana claims that when she is not online participating in social media activities, she is "actively obsessing" about social media activities and what she might be missing out on. The problem got so bad that she began to lose sleep at night, and she even found herself tuning out her children to think about the cyber world just a few mouse clicks away.

How did this happen? Grostern felt that because "there is no line to draw between my activities on the social media networks and my business . . . it's pretty hard to feel that if I'm not on 24/7, then I am essentially giving myself a free pass to failure."

This is a common fear among entrepreneurs. It is very easy to confuse yourself with your business. However, the business may not need breaks, but the human running the business must take breaks. It is not only acceptable but also necessary to unplug from the world—and especially from social media.

Grostern has made a pledge to control her social media addiction and has stuck to her goals. Here are a couple of her techniques for controlling her urges:

- **Get regular exercise.** Exercise provides your body with dopamine and endorphins, which are the same chemicals that flood your brain when you use social media. By creating an alternative source of these chemicals, you lessen your cravings to check Facebook or Twitter.

- **Set strict workday limits.** After "quitting time," she turns off her computer and mobile devices. This not only stops her from burning away leisure time, but it also encourages her to stay productive during the day.

CHAPTER 5

You Never Take a Break
or a Vacation from Work

WHY YOU ARE STUCK

You have a fear of falling behind or missing an opportunity. As discussed in the previous chapter, in this 24/7 connected world, you think the only way to compete is to be constantly available to customers and vendors. This is because you have a low confidence in your product, people, and distribution channels. You believe that your only competitive advantage is your superior service. But over the long run, this strategy is far too expensive and is physically exhausting. In this scenario, you or an employee has to constantly check all the methods of communication used with customers (phone, text, fax, email, and social media) all the time. With all these channels, you have a constant fear of getting left behind. This never leaves you any time to be with your family or focus on your favorite activities. In fact, when you are not at work, your mind is still at the office.

You think the business will collapse without you. You feel that you are the center of the business and all-important decisions need to go through you. There is no one else in your company who can run things without your close involvement. You have not set up a hierarchical organization, but rather a wheel where you are at the center and all the employees are spokes that only communicate directly with you. As a result, no one can really work any part of the business independently and you constantly have responsibility for all the critical tasks.

You read about how others have succeeded. You discover the latest entrepreneurial wunderkind like Snapchat was reportedly offered $3 billion from Facebook after being in business for only two years (and no revenue). You ask, why can't this be you? Aren't you as smart and work as hard as these guys? When your family and peers point out this same success story, it only makes you feel like more of a failure. As a result, you redouble your efforts to work harder, faster, and longer so you don't fall short the next time.

You let technology invade every part of your life. You are surrounded by it, and it keeps pushing you, prodding you to pay attention. There is a constant fear of getting left behind if you don't reply immediately to everything. As a result, you use your smartphone in the bedroom *and* bathroom. You know there is a cost for rush decisions, but the fear of not being involved is greater. Your smartphone is always on, and most of the time, it's in your hand. Even with in-person meetings, you are distracted by checking your phone. Like the average person, you check your phone more than times a day.[4]

There seems to be an endless amount of work. In small business, this is always true. With the influx of information and the resulting possibilities, there is an unlimited amount of work nipping at your heels. Because you have a very broad scope of business objectives, there seem to be so many possible directions to go at once. You are always busy but never really feel productive.

According to a survey by Good Technology, cited in *Digital Journal*, more than 80% of employees work an additional seven hours per week *outside the office*. In the survey of one thousand workers, 30% said they kept working because they found it "hard to switch off," 60% said they do it to stay organized, and 50% said they felt they had "no choice" but to work at home.

Because technology, such as smartphones and tablets, makes it so easy to stay connected, it can often feel like you have an obligation to stay up-to-date on work no matter where you are. This can be taken to comical extremes like the 50% of workers in the Good Technology survey who check their email while in bed!

This type of behavior takes a toll on your personal health. Dr. Helena Johnson of the Chartered Society of Physiotherapy says, "While doing a bit of extra work at home may seem like a good short-term fix, if it becomes a regular part of your evening routine, it can lead to problems such as neck or back pain [and] stress-related illness." A body that is always on alert, never truly gets to rest and renew.

HOW TO GET UNSTUCK

Build other competitive advantages. Responding 24/7 to customer and vendor requests is not a sustainable competitive advantage. There will always be a company that will spend more time to do it faster than you. Your business needs to develop other reasons why customers buy and remain loyal. Review the key leverage points in Chapter 1 because they can become long-term advantages.

Rather than the 24/7 approach, here are some other competitive advantages to develop:

People: Customers do business with people they know, like, and trust. If your company has these people, customers will stay and remain loyal. Most customers, even when they receive poor service, have a very high barrier to switching vendors. In other words, get the customer, make a personal connection, and they will almost never leave.

Product: If your brand is known for having a superior product, customers will only want to buy it and not be lured by competitors. In the short-term, this can be a large advantage. In extreme cases, like Apple, consumers wait a long time (even in line) to get the product they want.

Intellectual property: If you have a defendable patent, this may be a reason why competitors can't introduce a similar product to the market. While this can provide a long-term advantage, it can be an expensive proposition to defend, and expert legal advice needs to be employed.

Proprietary distribution agreements: In this case, customers are required to get the product exclusively through the authorized distributors you choose. This gives you control of who sells your product and to some extent, how it is priced.

Build real business value. If the business can't operate a day, or a week, without you, then there really is no long-term business value. Carol Roth, CNBC contributor and best-selling author of *The Entrepreneur Equation* says, instead, you have created a job but not a real company. As discussed in Chapter 1, hire skilled people for each position who can take responsibility for running that portion of the business on their own. Train them and have feedback loops in place so you can trust them. This can be tested with one person and then expanded to others as your confidence increases.

Stop comparing yourself. While this is inevitable, it is also very dangerous. I cringe every time the media heralds "success stories" like Instagram, which built a company in a short period of time and sold it to Facebook for billions of dollars. While I am excited for those owners, it really does a disservice to all other small business owners. It puts unrealistic goals in their heads and makes them feel inferior. Success stories like this are truly the outlier for the other twenty-eight million small businesses in the United States. Almost all the owners reading about the success of this company will never even remotely approach this type of financial success. In fact, according to the U.S. Small Business Administration, 75% of all small businesses don't even have a single employee. Instead, the best strategy is to stop comparing. Success is simply being able to financially support your family at something you enjoy doing. Measure yourself against goals that you and your employees set, not the ones touted by the media or your peers.

Focus on the critical work that must be done today and this week. No one can approach an endless pile of work. Push everything else out of your mind that does not need to be worked on today or this week. Identify the tasks that are in the critical path of achieving the long-term goal. As discussed in Chapter 4, set clear priorities based on your defined mission for this month or quarter. Sift all activities through these set goals and constantly ask, "Is this task really in the critical path?" If the answer is no, delete these non-"A" priorities off your to-do list and quickly forget them for today.

Take a break each day without work or technology. Technology constantly demands our attention. However, several strategies for regaining control of your life can work:

1. **Just turn it off.** At least once a day, do not let your smartphone or tablet enter a location where you regularly visit. This can be the gym, temple, restaurant, family dinner, outside walk, or other selected place. Make it a habit that does not get broken easily so that location can be a guaranteed daily "rest place."

2. **Never bring it to bed.** Depending on your age, many people bring their phones to bed. This is always a bad idea, except under extreme circumstances. Workplace dreams may enter your mind while sleeping, but your phone actually ringing shouldn't be a part of them. Most of the things that happen after work hours can wait until the next day without penalty.

3. **Leave it at the office.** For the past ten years, I have taken worldwide trips with my family. During some excursions that have lasted from two to four weeks, I keep my phone turned off. While I have missed a few great business opportunities, the recharged feeling from the con-

nection with my family and the places we visited more than made up for it. The first few times, this can be very scary. If this step is initially too drastic for you, alternate strategies can be used. For example, while on vacation, commit to only working designated hours during the day (early morning or late evening), then turn off the phone for the remainder of the time. Similarly, if you are on vacation for a week, pick two days to work and keep away from the phone and computer all the other times.

Stop leading separate lives. The most successful people have found a way to merge their personal and professional lives. Stop fighting against a strict separation. At the same time, find time to recharge daily where work never enters. This could be mealtime, bed time, at the gym or out for a run. Your family certainly does not appreciate you still being at the office when you're supposed to be having dinner or taking a vacation, and your body and mind do not appreciate it either. Leave your work at work—it's your business, so take ownership of it by leaving the work when you leave the office. You may find that by taking your mind off work while at home, you'll be less stressed and more productive during normal hours.[5] While all these strategies take discipline, they have a huge payoff by preventing the burnout that so often accompanies running a small business.

CASE STUDY

TAKING A TIME OUT

VALUE PROP INTERACTIVE

Bringing an entrepreneurial dream to life takes a lot of hard work. During busy times, there may be no such thing as a weekend, holiday, or vacation. Management consultant Jose Palomino had not taken a vacation in over a year and believed that he was "too busy" to get one. He finally figured out how to make taking a vacation a priority that actually *improved* his business.

Plan the vacation ahead of time. Vacations do not need to happen spontaneously, nor should they. Planning a vacation well in advance will give your business and clients plenty of time to adjust to your absence, and doing things like purchasing plane tickets and hotel reservations can serve as inducement to eliminate any lingering tasks or projects. According to a research article that Palomino read in *Convince and Convert,* "The effect of vacation anticipation boosted happiness for eight weeks." That's a nice incidental bonus to the "investment" of a vacation.

Know the benefits. Just "taking a break" does not seem like a productive use of time, but Palomino took care to do some research and consider the real pros of going on vacation. He discovered that by taking one, his employees would gain experience in the business by learning how to cope without constant guidance. He also found that a vacation provides a very useful shift in perspective to let him view old problems in a new way.

CHAPTER 6

You Take Dangerous Risks
Instead of Calculated Actions

WHY YOU ARE STUCK

You think success is about taking gigantic risks. The popular media loves to highlight people who take that big risk and succeed. Think Apple's iPad or Tesla electric cars. Business folklore is beset with stories like these:

In winter 2001, Tim Westergren, founder of Pandora Radio, was out of money. He faced a stark choice. Close the business, or find a way to keep going. He decided to keep the company alive by asking people to defer their salaries. Amazingly, more than fifty people agreed to defer $1.5 million over two years. He also adds that, "when we were finally rescued by an investment in 2004, I had maxed out eleven credit cards." Pandora become the revolutionary Internet radio app and spawned competitors like iTunes Radio.

James Dyson of vacuum cleaner fame, spent about six years developing 5,127 prototypes to get one to work the way he wanted. Unfortunately, during this process, each year he sank further into debt. After fourteen years, he owed about $4 million on multiple mortgages on his house. He says, "I repaid the bank loan within about four or five months of first selling the product. The bank kept using me in their advertising as an example of how they loan money!" In 2013, billionaire Dyson was ranked No. 286 on *Forbes* list of the world's richest people.

While the business landscape is littered with product launch failures and bankrupt companies, you choose to ignore them because it is much more rewarding to focus on the one entrepreneur-in-a-million like Amazon's Jeff Bezos or Starbucks' Howard Schultz who took big risks and succeeded. This is popular because it makes you believe, on a particularly bad day at the office, that if "Jeff and Howard did it," you can too.

You take swift actions only to satisfy your ego. You call yourself a calculating businessperson, but in reality, your actions more closely resemble a grudge. You have a tendency to put your personal bravado and agenda above your business's long-term objectives. Secretly, you are trying to prove to _____ (fill in the blank with your mother, spouse, children, friends, peers, or competitors) that you have the _____ (fill in the blank with chutzpah, audacity, courage, strength, or guts) to take that big risk to succeed. You have always dreamed of sponsoring a particular event or having a full-page ad in your favorite journal or website. You pound your chest by stating with conviction that big rewards require taking big risks. You remember the NFL coach that "went for it on the fourth down." (Even though, statistically, these only succeed about 60% of the time with one or two yards to go.) [6]

You want to live a life that is big, bold, and remarkable. Remember the Broadway musical, *Pippin*? You have made a profit at your company. So to take your business to the next level, you think you have to keep taking bigger risks. You reason the bigger the risk, the greater the ultimate glory. Additionally, you think the only way people will follow you is for you to show you are willing to "put it all on the line." You are more concerned with appearances and what people think than with what actually happens. You remind yourself that entrepreneurship is not for the faint of heart.

Too much money eventually makes you stupid. After some financial success, you finally have more money to invest in the company. But you waste your resources on purchases that don't impact the success of your company like swank furniture, beautiful office space, and fancy outdoor barbecue grills. You are too impatient to test smaller ideas and wait for the results. You'd rather "go big or go home." As a result, you direct your company to invest all your development or marketing money into one product launch or marketing campaign. You have no resources to follow up or change direction when the results come in. You invest blindly in this strategy where you do not know what success even looks like or how to measure your progress toward the best outcome.

You make cause-and-effect relationships where they do not exist. You are convinced when you do X, then Y happens. For example, you believe that since your best salesperson makes fifty calls a day, this is the reason why he sells the most. However, you have no data to back up this claim. Regardless, you instruct all the other salespeople to do the same thing. But surprisingly, they don't experience similar success and you don't know why.

HOW TO GET UNSTUCK

Big risk takers fail most of the time. The small business failure rate is enormous, with almost 44% failing in the first three years.[7] The rate is even higher for retail operations. Even big brands take risks and fail in the process.

As discussed in Chapter 2, Harley Davidson tried to get into perfume, but fans didn't go along for the ride. Colgate thought it could go from toothpaste to kitchen entrees. It must have been the taste! Life Savers wanted to add soda to what they sold, but consumers did not want to drink liquid candy. Ben Gay tried aspirin, but customers did not want to swallow anything that they sold. Apple's Newton tablet was too far ahead of its time. (In fact, handwriting technology has never caught on and has been replaced by touch screens.) People wanted to drink beer from Coors, not their water. Alcohol is social, but drinking water is not. Sony's expensive investment in Betamax was not enough to win the videocassette race to the longer format VHS. Apple and Android smartphones are now replacing the BlackBerry.

We never read about these failures because they don't make good headlines. In our society, we celebrate winners, not losers. (Well, we love to celebrate losers that have come back from failure, but only if they eventually succeed in a substantial way.)

The lesson here is not to fear failure but instead make smaller decisions so you have the energy and financial resources after each result to alter the course and try again. Iteration and practice eventually have a higher probability of success.

"When you find yourself in a hole, stop digging." This simple quote from cowboy Will Rodgers is important to every small business. Unfortunately, most owners go past the point of no return and waste additional money. This is when many ask for additional lines of credit, spend more of their life savings, or ask family members for cash. This happens because most owners believe they can sell their way out of any financial situation, but, in fact, it becomes more like a Ponzi scheme. That is, the owner is paying past debts with cash meant for future growth. This typically does not happen because cash resources limit the amount of time for the turn around. If sales and cash flow are both shrinking, this is an important time to stop and evaluate whether to take the company forward. As described in the Case Study in Chapter 7, Richard Melman, the successful restaurant entrepreneur who founded Lettuce Entertain You, has his success rooted in this concept. He knows when to close single restaurants if it is not successful, instead of keeping it open and burying his company with a single failure.

If first you don't succeed, try something else. Most small business successes are not based on the concept initially described in their business plan. For example, Scott Jordan, who started a travel clothing company, Scottevest, originally conceived his business as licensing its "technology enabled clothing" to other manufacturers. Only after listening to how his customers were using his products, was he able to see the travel-clothing niche his company really filled. In my third company, we sold technical software through a mail order catalog. When our vendors asked if they could advertise in the catalog, it created an entirely new revenue stream we had not anticipated in the business plan.

Check the ego at your office door. Many point to Donald Trump and HP's Carly Fiorina as famous examples of big CEO egos. Contrary to popular belief, successful entrepreneurs don't have big egos. Instead, they channel the quiet confidence of leaders like Tony Hsieh, the CEO of Zappos. "At the end of the day, Zappos ships shoes online. You can argue that isn't very sexy," says Eric Ryan, the innovative co-founder of Method Home Products. "But Hsieh has elevated everybody's work to a much more meaningful purpose. That's such a rare and powerful thing. Most CEOs tend to be strong operators, but he's a strong operator and a strong visionary. He's just a fresh model of what a modern businessperson should be—no ego and in it for the right reasons."

Before taking any action, think about the real reasons behind it. If the answer begins with "I want . . .," this is void of sound business reasoning. Then stop and find another answer. Most employees don't want to serve a person but a "higher common purpose." Many of the people I talk to who knew Steve Jobs say that he was horrible to work for. But they stayed at Apple, not for Jobs, but for his vision and what the company was able to achieve with him.

Take small and patient iterative steps. Only invest in what is trackable and repeatable. Gone are the days of investing money in marketing or other activities where the results are not known. Before taking an action, determine what will be the lesson, regardless of whether it succeeds or fails. Write down specifically what success or failure will look like. When the result is known, determine what needs to be done next. Are you off-course or moving in the right direction? Did you predict correctly, or were your assumptions wrong? At that point, the most important element is labeling the outcome not as a success or failure, but rather what can be learned, if anything. Remember, in a small business, small actions can easily be corrected with little effort and resources. Success in business is very much like tacking across a windy lake. While the captain wants to go directly toward the goal, they typically need to zigzag back and forth according to wind patterns.

In business, these patterns are marketplace forces that influence the direction of your company. They are traditionally the pains that your customers will pay to alleviate or the products offered by competitors. The path your company takes really is not relevant. The only thing that matters is achieving the goal. Many companies started building one product, and after a number of years, now do something totally different. For example, phone manufacturer Nokia started out making rubber tires and boots in 1865. Ball Corp. became famous for its canning jars before going into aerospace. Nintendo sold playing cards before it attracted customers to its video games.

CASE STUDY
BACK TO THE BASICS
I CAN HAS CHEEZBURGER

Entrepreneurship is a gamble. Small business owners take risks to succeed, but sometimes they get reckless, and that is when trouble happens.

In 2000, when Ben Huh was only twenty-two years old, he raised $750,000 in the middle of the dot-com bubble to fund his own start-up company, Raydium, a software analytics firm. He had very little experience in business management, but he took the risk, rolled the dice, and lost big time.

In just eighteen months, Raydium was flat out of cash. Not only that, but the dot-com crash had arrived and the few investors he'd connected with to raise his first round of capital were not about to invest again. Huh's big risk to start a completely new company was a failure.

But six years later, Huh tried again, still taking a risk, but a smaller one this time. Instead of starting a brand-new company, he bought the established humor blog "I Can Has Cheezburger" alongside a team of angel investors he had brought together ahead of time. From there, he parlayed "I Can Has Cheezburger" into a ninety-employee company and a network of humor blogs with twenty-five million unique visitors a month.

Risk taking is inevitable in entrepreneurship. But the most successful entrepreneurs know that oftentimes, it's better to take the surer odds than the bigger payout.

CHAPTER 7

You Think the Only Alternative to Success Is Failure

WHY YOU ARE STUCK

You think failure is not an option. You are afraid of being a called a failure. As a result, you resolve never to quit or surrender regardless of the circumstances. You can never admit that it makes no financial sense to continue in your business. You keep going even when you agree with your advisors that you have very little chance of success. Calling it quits would bring the shame of failure, and you can't face it. This should never have happened to you. With all your education and experience, you think you should be in a different place. In fact, you don't want to end this company because you have no idea of what to do in the future.

You think success is a straight line. As discussed in Chapter 6, you believe that success breeds more success. You think that company and career success are linear lines going up and to the right. I also believed this because when growing up, my mother told me that every year I would be promoted and make more money. You believe this because it is the way every successful story seems to be told in the press and social media. When a successful company retells their tale of their beginning, any failure seems to be part of the original plan.

Fear takes hold. You are so conditioned to not make a mistake, rather than to take a chance, that fear begins to paralyze you. Being stuck starts to lead to diminished returns and bad outcomes. Your fear of failure, in fact, is a self-fulfilling prophecy. Amateur golfers who are afraid to hit their ball in the sand trap usually do. With so much focus on not failing, you meet your expectations and fail most of the time. As Earl Nightingale in *The Strangest Secret* said, "You are what you think about." This is the same principle the more modern-day, *The Secret,* by Rhonda Byrne, is based on.

I actually used my customer's fear of failure to make sales early in my career. When I was at IBM in the 1980s, they told us "no one ever got fired for buying IBM." This concept helped because I had to sell against competitors whose products seemed technologically similar to ours but always much cheaper. I frequently used a technique that was called "FUD" (fear, uncertainty, and doubt) to direct the decision maker to buy IBM. In my sales calls, I recounted all the things that could go wrong if he chose a competitor. Fortunately, the decision maker many times chose IBM, despite the fact that we were more expensive, because we were perceived as the low-risk alternative.

You stop taking risks. You are so adverse to failure that you only go after the easy wins. You begin thinking very tactically and try to grind out daily sales. Practically, you can't afford to take any risks because cash flow is so tight. In reality, you have so little confidence that any rejection sends you into a psychological tailspin and you are unable to bounce back quickly. This happens in many Asian cultures. A.A. Gill, a British newspaper columnist, reflects about how Japanese culture affects the way that business is done there:

"A Japanese man tells me that the key to understanding Japan is to grasp that it is a shame-based culture. In the West, success is the carrot. In Japan, fear of failure and ostracism is the stick. This isn't merely a semantic difference; it's a basic mindset. Westerners trying to do business here complain that it is impossible to get decisions made. The Japanese negotiate for months without saying yes or no. Nobody wants to lay his face on the line; there is no comeback from failure. Decisions emerge out of group inertia. Japan manages to be both rigidly hierarchical and enigmatically lateral."

HOW TO GET UNSTUCK

Remember that failure is an acceptable option. In April 1970, when things went terribly wrong aboard the Apollo 13 spacecraft, astronaut Jim Lovell told mission control there was a problem. In response to getting the spacecraft home safely, Gene Kranz, the flight director, famously told his team, "failure is not an option." His words were memorialized the 1995 movie, *Apollo 13*, and it has become the rallying cry for many sports teams, politicians, and companies. Unfortunately, these words don't hold true for small business owners. You don't need a crystal ball to figure this out that failure is in everyone's past and future. Fortunately, America is one of the few places in the world where businesspeople get multiple chances to come back from failure. Bankruptcy law in the United States is relatively permissive. In the 1830s, when Alexis de Tocqueville and Gustave de Beaumont were given an eighteen-month leave to study the penal system in the America, they were surprised to learn that we did not have debtor prisons as in England, where if you did not pay all your bills you went to jail. Other cultures perceive that in America, businesspeople are allowed to fail and recover. Colin Jones, a professor at the University of Tasmania, observes, "In America, failing is part of the educational process of becoming an entrepreneur."

This is not the way it is in other parts of the world. As I describe in my book, *Bounce*, Vietnamese refugee Andria Lieu believed that "failure means that I'm not strong enough, that I'm weak, and that I'm not smart enough." Today, Andria runs a very successful clothing company in Chicago. Her attitude is reflected in many Asian countries—when you financially fail at business, you are literally forced to move out of your city, region, or country because the stigma of failure looms so large. A student in a class that I was speaking to at the Thunderbird School of Global Management in 2005 described how her parents left Taiwan after her father failed. In order to have any future, she explained that they had to leave.

Learn new definitions of failure. I can still picture my younger son forming an "L" with his thumbs and forefingers in front of his head to make fun of a team that lost. The expressions business owners used to describe failure can even be worse: bust, deficiency, dud, fiasco, nobody, sinking ship, washout, and wreck. In Yiddish, someone who fails is called a *nebbish*—literally translated as "a nothing." The language we use influences feelings and actions. Learning to call failure something neutral, like decision point, disappointment, outcome, or result, will help you move forward. As former President Bill Clinton said, "Defeat is never final."

Be afraid, and do it anyways. I took a few Dale Carnegie classes when I was training with IBM. One of the best things that I learned was how to harness my fear of failure. I still can get sick to my stomach over fear. Some people characterize it as "butterflies in the stomach," but to me, they feel more like wasps. The Dale Carnegie class did not teach me techniques to eliminate that fear but instead taught me to teach the "butterflies to fly in formation." Remember, it is acceptable to be afraid, but then you must take the action anyway. Using fear and teaching it to "fly in formation" may not produce the perfect outcome, but it gets you moving to a different place where a new set of actionable decisions can be made. As Robert Frost said, "The only way out is through."

Choose a place to put this into practice. For me, I hate to fly, but I am on an airplane almost every week. I fly because I love speaking to small business owners. The "getting there" can be a very fearful part. I deal with my fear of flying by channeling it somewhere else. I use high-energy music on my iPhone to redirect all the airplane bumps in a kind of seated series of dance moves. I even use a playlist called "Turbulence Tunes" to help with the process.

I also practice techniques every morning when I have to test my blood sugar as a result of having diabetes since 1995. At the start of every day, I am literally tested. I prick my finger to see if my blood sugar is in the normal range of 80 to 120 mg/dl to avoid complications. Most mornings I fail and feel shame. But I have learned to think about how I can improve, let go of this one test, and try to do better on the next one. Avoiding testing my blood sugar would not help me control my diabetes.

Remember, there is always a choice. And alternatives bring multiple satisfactory outcomes. For example, when considering selling a new product, a company can:

1. *Develop and distribute the product themselves.* This means doing everything internally.

2. *Source the product through another manufacturer and distribute it themselves.* This means not "reinventing the wheel" but using a business partner that already has an effective product in the marketplace.

3. *Develop the product and have others distribute the product.* This means hiring a distribution channel so your company can focus on developing and manufacturing the best product.

4. *Don't develop or distribute the product.* This means choosing not to be involved with the product at all.

Since there is likely not a single answer that fits every situation, always think about multiple best-case alternatives to any path.

Face it: "The worst they can do is eat you, and that is illegal." My attorney Zane Smith always reminded me of this on particularly bad days in my business career. Face what needs to come next over and over again. Forget if someone else would have done it differently or better. It's OK to be afraid, then to move forward anyway. Failure is never a desired outcome, but it gets you unstuck and forces you to move on to a new place—where you will always find new opportunities to succeed.

CASE STUDY

MAKING FRIENDS WITH FAILURE

LETTUCE ENTERTAIN YOU RESTAURANTS

Restaurateur and entrepreneur Richard Melman is the founder of the highly successfully Lettuce Entertain You Enterprises (LEYE), a group of ninety restaurants across the United States. Most of these restaurants are one-of-a-kind concepts, from the burger-slinging focus of Epic Burger to the original comedic "mean servers" gimmick of the famous Ed Debevics. Thanks to Melman's instincts, LEYE grosses nearly $200 million a year. Through hard work and persistence, he has managed to turn many of his restaurants into successes.

However, Melman is no stranger to failure. Sometimes, the only smart thing to do is to let something die. The iconic black mark in his portfolio is "The Great Gritzbe's Flying Food Show." The restaurant had been a moderate success and was facing the final year of its lease. In an attempt to boost business, Melman rechristened the restaurant "Not So Great Gritzbe's" and apparently decorated the place with posters of Tums, Alka-Seltzer, and indigestion jokes.

According to Melman, customers got the joke, and then went to eat elsewhere. "Not So Great Gritzbe's" closed its doors six months later, and he admitted, "That was stupid."

In an interview with FoodArts.com, Melman said, "I worry about my kids because they've opened three smashing successes. I'm not sure success is the best teacher."

CHAPTER 8

Your Customers Can't Find You

WHY YOU ARE STUCK

Prospects have no idea who you are and what you can offer them. You have not clearly described the pain you can heal for them. Your company does not stand out from all the other business offerings out there. You have no memorable brand. When asked what your company does, current customers have no clear or compelling answer.

You are marketing where customers can't find you. You have no comprehensive or long-term marketing strategy. You let others drive the choices for your business or let other vendors' salespeople sell you want they want. You never follow up to see the results of any marketing campaign. In fact, you have a knee-jerk reaction to marketing expenses as you increase and lower this category at will. You once had a marketing manager, but after a month, you fired him due to a lack of results. Now, you mostly think that marketing is a waste of money. You have not taken the time to find out where customers are discussing the problems your company solves.

Your business never gets in the "maybe pile." When a typical customer is looking to buy a product or service, they put together a list of a few possible companies they could do business with. If your company is on that list, you will be chosen 33% of the time. But your company is not on that list because of how you market as described above.

HOW TO GET UNSTUCK

Establish a brand. Many small business owners ask this same question. Whether they are a plumber, lawyer, or landscape architect, they question why they really need a brand. To them, it seems like a waste of time and money since they insist that customers already know who they are. Furthermore, they are too busy finding customers to focus on building a brand!

In this increasingly crowded business world, it is very difficult to stand out from other companies. Access to the Internet, coupled with next-day shipping, has removed most distribution barriers, and many products have become commodities. To most consumers, many companies provide similar products or services, so they just search for the lowest price. A company's brand ensures their value will stand out from their competitors. It also helps that company "get found" when a customer is shopping. It makes them memorable to the consumer.

In any economy, people buy when they are in pain and have the money to solve it. Any marketing activity a company executes consistently ensures the business can get found when the customer is ready to buy. If the customer can't find the company, they have no chance of being chosen. A consumer has to consider that company (i.e., put them in the "maybe" pile) to get a sale. If most successful companies are chosen more than 33% of the time they are considered by a customer, then the key to growing a business is to get considered by more shopping customers.

Don't confuse your brand with your logo. A brand separates your company from your competitors. Buying is an emotional experience. What will the customer see and feel when interacting with your company? The brand is what the company is known for, the pain it solves, and its values. Alternately, a logo is just a graphical representation of the company's name. While the logo can be recognizable, it's not the brand.

Consumers will pay more for company brands that add value. For example, what comes to mind when a consumer thinks of Apple? The company is known for innovative, hip, easy-to-use, and expensive technology. This is evident in all of Apple's products and stores. For consumers, their brand clearly adds more value because consumers always pay a premium for them. In this way, Steve Jobs and his team built one of the most successful companies in the world. Similarly, Starbucks' brand is not just about selling coffee. They are seen as a warm and friendly atmosphere where customers can stay awhile to work alone or meet with others.

Use your brand to distinguish your company from its competitors.

It is what your prospects and customers think and feel when they come into contact with your business. Consumers stay loyal to brands they buy and remember which makes it harder for them to switch to a competitor. Developing a brand is an investment. Here are five steps to start developing an effective company brand.

1. *State why your business is important to customers.* Complete the following sentence:

   "My company helps _____ who are _____. "

For the first blank, fill in your perfect customer. Who are they? Narrow this down as much as possible. In the second blank, fill in the problem your company specifically solves. For example, for me, "My company helps small business owners get unstuck."

Similarly, Johnson Heating and Air helps homeowners whose heat is broken. Rebecca Maslin helps parents whose children don't sleep well. All these examples target a specific type of prospect and their individual problem.

2. *Why is your company the best?* Complete the following sentence:

   "My company is the best at _____!"

Many companies will say customer service, but this is not a differentiator because so many small businesses promise this, and few are truly able to deliver. If you are stuck coming up with the answer, ask your customers what adjectives they use to describe your company. Why did they choose to buy from you at the beginning? Why do they continue to be your customer? When they talk about your product, what do they say? Is it your unique product or service offering? Is your company the fastest, smartest, or most knowledgeable? Take time to brainstorm with multiple employees and customers for the answer to this question. Do the answers match, or are they different? If they are not the same, this will lead you to question what your brand image in the market really is.

3. *Test the brand in front of your employees and customers.* Does your brand ring true for both of them? Do your products and all your actions around it truly reflect your brand inside and outside the company? If it does not, this is the time to make adjustments. Many companies say their brand is one thing, but their actions don't reflect it. In the world of social media, company authenticity is becoming an increasing requirement. For example, if an insurance company says they are "always there for their customers," but every time any customer calls, they need to hold for thirty minutes; this hurts the brand's authenticity, and it will likely be publicized for all to see in customers' social media circles.

4. *Practice your brand.* Can everyone in your company state your brand? When asked, do they all say the same thing? Teach all employees the exact answer to this question: What does your company do (as discussed in number 1)? Put the brand message on the wall or on the desks in your office. Is every action your company takes consistent with that brand? Or do you say one thing and your employees do another?

The best way to learn branding is from looking at the success and failures of other well-known companies. Here are what some popular brands stand for and why it works or doesn't work:

- *General Electric (GE):* "Diversity and leading research in everything they do." *Why it works:* They make light bulbs, refrigerators, and airplanes. And they also lend money. They integrate themselves into every part of business and a consumer's life.

- *Coca-Cola:* "Deliciously fun." *Why it works:* They always hit the "pulse" of the local culture. Drinking Coke (while not good for your health) is somehow fun and invigorating!

- *BMW:* "Driving is fun for an elite few." *How it works:* They target young adults gaining wealth. They make cars that cater to these people like great interiors, sports handling, and technology gadgets.

- *UPS:* "Dependable" *How it works:* Can you recognize those brown trucks? While they are not the cheapest option for deliveries, they are very reliable when compared to the post office.

- *Syfy:* "The science fiction channel" *Why it doesn't work:* Originally they changed their name to separate themselves from their competitors, but unfortunately "syfy" is slang for syphilis.[8] It also means zits and filth. All these things are not positive associations for their brand.

- *Fifth Third Bank:* Confused? *Why it doesn't work:* When these two banks, the Third National Bank and Fifth National Bank of Cincinnati, merged, they came up with a new name. Unfortunately, many people are confused since they call it Third Fifth Bank (3/5ths)

- *Plantronics:* What do they sell? *Why it doesn't work:* The brand name does not reflect the product the company sells. Most people think its electronics for plants (not what they really sell, which are telephone headsets).

- *Colgate:* Kitchen entrées. *Why it doesn't work:* Here is a case where a brand name is so connected to one thing (toothpaste and other dental needs) that it is nearly impossible to make the jump. Can you imagine having Colgate food for dinner? Customers couldn't, and they withdrew the product.

- *Life Savers:* Soda. *Why it doesn't work:* While they produce three million rolls of candy a year, they were not able to make the transition to soda. Their name made consumers think they would be drinking "liquid candy." Customers did not buy it.

Find out where prospects are discussing their issues and problems

Go to these places first:

- *Google, Yahoo! or Bing search:* Search for customer problems that your company targets. For example, if your company repairs cars, search for phrases like "When is a car totaled?", "Will that dent rust?", and "Should I use original parts for my car repairs?" Comment on discussions that are happening within those search results.

- *Set up internet alerts.* Use alerts to notify you when new content appears in these areas or when someone mentions your company on the web. Free alerts are available through Google Alerts or paid services can be tracked with Dex Media.

- *Industry magazines, blogs, podcasts, or forums:* Find out what the most popular and active ones are in your industry. Again, these can be found through internet searches and customer or social media referrals.

- *Industry trade shows:* When attending shows, ask what people read and refer to most often for help with their businesses. Many times, shows will now have a Twitter hashtag, which can provide additional information (see "Twitter hashtag conversations" below).

- *Facebook page:* Search this social media tool to find relevant business pages. For example, if you are a florist, search for pages that discuss holidays and other life events (Valentine's Day, Mother's Day, funerals, and weddings).

- *Twitter hashtag conversations:* Search for popular hashtags to identify relevant conversations. Offer expert advice as part of these conversations and meet possible new long-term prospects.

- *LinkedIn groups:* Search for industry-related groups your company can join—and become part of those conversations. For example, if you run a plumbing company, you should join the "Contractor Discussion Group. For Plumbers, Electricians, Remodelers, Roofers, HVAC, and Handyman."

- *Pinterest boards:* Search and add relevant boards to your home feed. For example, a search for interior design produces hundreds of boards.

- *Google hangouts:* Sign up for relevant conversations and join them live, in person. While you can't search for hangouts you are not invited to, you can learn about them through the resources described above or go to www.gphangouts.com.

- **Track specific prospect discussions online.** Set up Twitter lists and Facebook interest groups to monitor specifically selected prospects, customers, and competitors' online content. This is helpful since it is nearly impossible to fully read any social media feeds for everyone that you follow. Using these customized private lists, it's easier to read and comment each time someone in your watch groups posts new content. Twitter also gives users the ability to sign up for other people's public lists, which can be helpful as well.

CASE STUDY

THE INCREDIBLY SUCCESSFUL COMPANY NO ONE EVER HEARD OF WHERE 2 GET IT

By any measure, Where 2 Get It, a location-based digital marketing company, was a huge success. CEO Manish Patel had built a business with more than five hundred clients in fifteen different industries. But if a company representative did not contact a prospect directly, Where 2 Get It could not be found.

In 2013, the company took actions to remedy this problem. They strategically analyzed their SEO and SEM performance and devised new tactics to improve their web performance. They increased their ad spend by 30% and optimized their online footprint through a website refresh and social media participation.

Although Where2GetIt is an online brand, it also participated in offline tactics such as trade shows, speaking engagements, and direct mail to become part of customer conversations. However, their real focus was on branded content, which Where2GetIt knew would be the key to being found. Content at Where2GetIt has become the foundation and success factor for inbound marketing. They first created content to align with their business goals and objectives. Next, they developed a strategic distribution plan and targeted it where their customers were: social, influential bloggers, and niche, industry magazine sites.

CHAPTER 9

Your Fear of Rejection Stops You from Selling

WHY YOU ARE STUCK

You don't want to think of yourself as a salesperson. You didn't start your company to sell things to customers. You classify yourself as an introvert and inherently shy. Your vision was that someone else would handle that part of the company. You thought sales would be relatively easy because you believe customers always buy the "best" product in the marketplace. In fact, you believe your product is so groundbreaking and superior, that it should really sell itself. You scratch your head and wonder why customers are not rushing to buy it. Your only answer is to continually go back to product development.

You dislike salespeople. When you think of a salesperson, you picture the experience of buying a used car, and you don't want to be labeled pushy, slimy, or aggressive like a car salesman. Besides, cold calling is just plain tacky. You imagine yourself calling people when they are right in the middle of something else. You think you are pushing them to buy things they don't need. In your mind, salespeople really serve no purpose since customers will automatically buy the best product in the marketplace. In fact, you believe the only thing salespeople seem to do well is collect overpaid commissions for little effort. From your viewpoint, they are not consistently in the office like the rest of the team. Some words you use to describe them are greedy, lazy, and brash. You would like to eliminate all the salespeople on your team, but you don't want to face the headache of the termination process.

You are afraid of the word "no." You have tried to sell, but you view it as a personal rejection when prospects decline to buy your product or service. So much of your self-worth is tied up in your company, you reason that if they liked you, they would buy from you. The last thing you want is to be involved in more activities that will sink your self-esteem. Your ego is bruised already from trying to make the other parts of the company work. As a result, you stop actively selling, or it becomes a very low priority that there never seems to be enough time for. You do whatever you can not to be involved in the actual selling. You desperately outsource all sales-related tasks to an unqualified manager, group of people, or company just to be rid of it. You are more comfortable when you can point to a box on the organization chart where all sales activity resides.

You stop asking customers to buy. You would much rather keep developing products and never bring them to the market. You may give them away for free (you call it a "beta launch") or "sell them" to customers you know well. You shy away from your products being tested by true product demand in the marketplace. This happens when you love your idea too much and refuse to change original or current market assumptions. While this type of "sales" is not very profitable, it is much easier on your ego and self-confidence. This is one of the main reasons many entrepreneurs never move beyond the business plan and prototyping stage. Business theory is always easier than the real world.

You don't even monitor sales activity. You justify this by saying it's not your expertise and this area is better without you. Your strength is in product development, manufacturing, or servicing the customer. Without measurement systems in place, you have no idea if the sales team that will yield future success is performing the right activities. You throw up your hands and remain helpless. As a result, you continue to hire and trust sales managers and people who are incompetent at what they do. When they don't get results, you blame it on them and not on your lack of knowledge of how to manage this area. You reason that you are potentially paying them huge amounts of money to succeed, so why aren't they successful. Instead, you fire them and hire another person. While you hope for the best, your sales team instead becomes a revolving door of different people, unattainable goals, and unproven methods.

HOW TO GET UNSTUCK

Realize sales is your job. Make no mistake: Every business owner sells, especially in start-ups or businesses with less than $5 million in sales. Remember, selling is not "beneath you" but instead a critical part of your job. If you don't want to sell, go make a career at another company so you can focus only on your narrow job description. Your personal ability to sell your own products and ideas internally to your staff is critical in building a team. In fact, it's key to your company's first few years of success.

If you can sell internally to employees, you make the transition to selling to paying customers. Forget the image of the used car salesman. There are plenty of salespeople who are liked and adored by their customers. Besides, being passionate is not the same as being pushy.

Break it down. For many small business owners, selling is easier if you break the task into small pieces:

- **Why are you so passionate that people should buy your product?** Think about why you got into this business in the first place. Typically, it would solve a pain that existed in the market. All customers love people who are passionate about their products—it shows you're authentic.

- **Identify if the prospect has the pain your product solves.** If they have this pain, then by demonstrating how your product can help them, you are doing them a big service. In your mind, focus on how your product will reduce their pain, bring pleasure, or save them money.

- **You need to be paid.** It is acceptable to be paid for helping cus-tomers. In fact, people value a product or service more when they have paid for it. There is nothing "dirty" about this voluntary form of market capitalism.

- **Quickly accept a "no" and move on.** Not every customer accepts that they have the pain your product solves or want to be helped right now. That's OK. Accept it and find someone who will ap-preciate your product.

Remember, rejection is never personal. In fact, it is not about you at all. When a prospect says "no" to your product or service, it means they do not have enough pain to want to change or they don't have the money to fix it right now.[9] Ultimately, it has nothing to do with you or your company. It does not mean you have an inferior product or that you are a bad person. In fact, many times the prospect chooses to do nothing at all and remains stuck. They do not even move forward with one of your competitors. This is because the pain for change or the money to finance it inside the company is not there yet. Alternately, it could also mean that you are not talking to a decision maker. Remember, no matter how hard you work or who you know, there are so many things beyond your con-trol. The sooner you realize that, the less frustrated you'll be. Work hard at the things you can control and learn to react decisively to factors that are out of your control.

Separate yourself from your company. It is difficult for many small business owners to separate their personal identity from their businesses. It seems harder for men because traditionally more of their self-worth came from their career, whereas women tended to focus more on their family. For many men, their value directly relates to how much mon-ey they earn to support their family. In conversations, men continually use this as a yardstick of their success and self-confidence. Humility will help make the separation between work and your self-esteem easier. This means not personally taking the entire blame for things that fall apart. Maybe failure resulted from fate, your team, or just bad luck. Develop enough humility to cut yourself some slack when things go horribly wrong. That also means not taking yourself so seriously during the highs so that you don't add to the pain of the lows. When you aren't so tied to your company's success and failure, it will also be easier to take the small risks needed to succeed.

Form the Help Department. Forget everything you ever knew about selling. Good salespeople are not pushy or slimy. Instead, they are educational and helpful. With this new mindset, you can take any fear out of selling. Think of this company function as the "Help Department," instead of the "Sales Department." If the prospect does not want to be "helped," then your job is to find another prospect that does. You can't help someone who doesn't want to help themselves. I discuss in Chapter 11 exactly how to do this.

Treat your salespeople like a respected and valued part of the team. In 1946, *Parade Magazine* publisher Arthur "Red" Motley said, "Nothing happens until a sale is made." He was 100% right. Nothing is done in any company without someone first selling something. Sales is the lifeblood of every company. Professional salespeople are always a highly skilled and respected part of the team—and they should be treated as such. Unfortunately, many company cultures form around jealously disparaging them even when they are successful.

However, if their compensation plan is set right, either they will be the highest paid people in the company (based on their success) or the lowest paid (based on their failure). They can even make more money than the top brass. And they have a right to— because salespeople take a risk with their compensation when they agree to be paid a very low base. In exchange, when they are successful, they make a lot of money. They should never be criticized for huge commissions. Most other employees are guaranteed their salary, with a very small bonus of 3%-5%. They never face the same type of risk with their salary or scrutiny for results as salespeople do daily.

Depending on your company's gross margin, selling expenses need to be 10%-20% of your revenue. Look at the commission as a percentage of the lifetime value (LTV) of a customer, instead of just a percentage of current sales. For example, if the company has a 50% gross margin and the average customer stays for three years with an annual sale of $100 per year, then every sale brings in $150 of gross profit (50% of $100 = $50 x 3). If a salesperson gets a 10% commission on a $100 sale, then the company is paying $10 for $150 of gross profit. Not a bad deal when you look at it that way.

CASE STUDY
USING REJECTION TO MAKE MONEY
COMPUVOX

In the early 1990s, I joined a company called CompuVox with two people I found from a classified section of the newspaper. My company responsibilities were focused on sales. At that time, this meant following up with prospects by phone or snail mail to show them a product demo. On a daily basis, I had to do cold calling, which involved a lot of rejection. This came in the form of leaving voice mails that were never returned or talking to gatekeepers who never let you through to the decision maker. To hit my projected numbers, I had to dial the phone almost one hundred times a day. This was a difficult task sitting in an office by myself day after day.

I finally developed a strategy to overcome this. I positioned a picture of my family in front of my phone. I realized, if I did not dial the phone, I could not support them. I then figured out how many calls it took to get someone on the phone. I calculated how many calls equaled a sale and what I was paid for each sale. Doing the math, I realized I was getting paid $2.50 each time I dialed the phone, regardless if I made a connection. This helped me realize that rejection was just another way to make money. Fast forward to today's methods of relationship selling. Sending valuable email messages or social media comments can be mathematically calculated in the same way to help you get over your fear.

CHAPTER 10

You Keep Calling People Who Don't Respond

WHY YOU ARE STUCK

You keep contacting "big fish" that never reply. You have worked hard going on a series of big sales calls. You are excited that they finally said yes and they want to get started next week. You congratulate yourself that all the effort has finally paid off. As agreed, you call them next week at the predetermined time. Surprisingly, they are not there. What's even stranger is when they don't call you back immediately. Instead, you email them, but again you hear nothing. You anxiously call and email them every few days, but there is no reply. Now, you are getting nervous because this sale is so critical to your company's success. This is the customer everyone has been waiting for and will take your business to the next level. You reason that this is just a temporary setback and are confident that their order will still come through very soon.

The "done deal" becomes a "no deal." Ultimately, after months of calling, either you never hear back from the customer or they keep delaying their purchase. You begin to wonder what you did wrong to make this happen. You reason that if you can only fix this one little thing, the customer will renew their interest and finally buy your product. You think that consistently "bugging them" will make a difference. You keep calling, emailing, and sending letters. You have even tried to show up at their company unannounced with an appreciation gift, but you can't get in to see them. With all this activity, hope, and worry occupying your brain, it prevents you from talking to other prospects that may be interested. You still believe that you are just one returned phone call away from making that big sale.

HOW TO GET UNSTUCK

Think about it. Was that really a "yes"? I find that when I go on sales calls with business owners, our interpretation of what actually happened at the meeting can sometimes be drastically different. They sometimes tell me the meeting went extremely well and the customer is ready to buy. What I saw was a small business owner who talked too much about his or her own solution and never really identified what the customer needed. Just because a prospect lets you babble on about your company, doesn't mean they will buy your product. Many customers are just too polite or bored to interrupt you in a meeting.

Go back and replay in your mind what was actually said. Any assumptions will hurt you here. Did they agree that your product matches their pain by making a declarative statement like "I think your product can really work at our company"? Did you identify how much they would pay to solve the pain, like mentioning an actual dollar figure? Did they say they wanted to buy today or set a particular time frame of less than a month? Did they say they personally had the money or budget to buy the product? If not all these questions were answered, then you are not even close to a sale.

Forget maybe. Many times what the customer actually said was they might be interested sometime in the future. This type of "maybe" is a silent killer in the sales process. You hate confrontations, so you don't push for a "yes" or "no" to any of your questions. You think "maybe" gives you hope and will alleviate the pressure of making more prospecting calls (which you dislike). Remember that "maybe" is really a "no, not now" from a prospect that doesn't have the courage, courtesy, or money to say they are not interested immediately. Prospects hate confrontations as much as you. Unfortunately, this type of reply keeps you hoping you can sell something to the prospect soon. This form of thinking is one of the fastest ways to destroy your company. While "hope" may be good for long-term visions and missions, it has no place in the sales process. Renowned sales trainer Rick Page even titled his book *Hope Is Not a Strategy*. Every action should be based on factual Q&A's with prospects, not what you want them to do, or how you thought they replied. This is why it is good to have two people on a sales call, to review what actually happened. The goal here is not to sell the prospect "something," but rather to sell them one of your products or services that will solve a deep pain they have. "Soon" is not a length of time that can be forecasted since it is different for every prospect. People who are not really interested or don't want to make a decision use words like "soon," "later," or "in the near future."

Pass on "yes," and channel "Dr. No." Learn that when selling to a prospect, the second best answer is "no." In fact, force a quick "no" if possible by asking these questions:

- *Why do you specifically think that my product (or service) is a good fit?* Any prospect that is really interested in buying now should be able to answer this question.

- *What are the alternatives to buying my product?* Any prospect would have thought through all the alternatives before making a decision.

- *Do you have the budget to pay for this product?* Buyers know where the money is coming from.

- *What real financial value will you get from purchasing this product?* Buyers know how to justify any decision in monetary terms.

- *What will other people in your company think when you buy this product?* Buyers will anticipate objections from their peers.

While these questions will be difficult to ask (and even harder to listen for an answer), if a prospect can't affirmatively answer these questions, their "yes" is really "maybe." It will never survive the scrutiny when they seek approval to write a check or are asked questions by their peers or manager. If you get a hard "no" now, it saves a long process that will end in exactly the same place. Most important, it releases you to find other customers who truly want to buy from you now. Customers who say they want to buy later will not help meet sales goals or pay bills this month.

I thought you were dead. Many small business owners need help letting go of a very promising prospect. How long should you wait until letting them go? Contact the customer who you thought said "yes," a few times over the first two weeks. If you do not get a reply, wait a month and contact them again. If no reply is received, send them this email for the best results:

Email Title: Should we really work together?

Dear John,

I have been unsuccessful in my attempts to reach you and provide the information you requested. This typically means:

1. You've just been busy but are still very interested in talking with me about how I can help.

2. You are no longer interested, and I should stop trying to contact you.

Being a businessperson, I know you can appreciate the position I'm in, because you want to know similar answers from your customers. I want to provide you with excellent customer service and all the information you require to make an educated decision that will benefit your business. What I don't want to do is bother you with something if you are no longer interested. Could you please help both of us by letting me know which of the two situations we are in? This will allow me to better allocate my time while still providing you with the amount of attention you desire.

Thanks again,

Barry

With this letter, you will get a response 80% of the time from the prospect. This works because it encourages the prospect to say "no" in simple business terms they understand. This lets them off the sales hook easily if they were afraid of saying "no" after saying "yes" or after not replying to you for a long time. Remember, it is far too costly to do business with anyone who doesn't truly want to do business with you.

To increase the odds of a reply to 95%, a slightly risky letter can be sent. At this stage, however, I recommend using it since there is not much to lose.

Email Title: I thought you were dead!

Dear John,

I really don't know what else to say. I thought we had some good conversations about working together. I am personally surprised and a bit disappointed I have not heard from you. Maybe you are no longer at Pennewig Company, or you are sick or were in a serious accident. These different possibilities make me worry about you. At this point, I truly don't care if we do business together, but let me know that you are OK or if you have taken a job at a different company.

Thanks for taking the time to respond,

Barry

Remember that any response is the ultimate goal. You may not do business with this prospect, but you will get a reply, and this will help you move onto other prospects. On the small chance that none of these methods generates a reply, cross them off your active list and place them back into suspect funnel.

Practice the "Rapid Release" strategy. A key to being successful in sales is to focus on the prospects that truly want to buy and have the money to solve their pain with your product. The worst part is the waiting and not letting go of the opportunity is hurting your overall sales efforts. Psychologically, you are afraid to let go of this opportunity, and it prevents you from pursuing others. But when you only focus on "now" prospects, you cut your sales effort by 50%, ultimately increasing your results. For example, if you contact 5 people a day, or 100 a month, your current close rate is 20%. That gives you a yield of twenty customers. Unfortunately, 25 of these 100 prospects have long ago stopped responding to your queries (and are no longer qualified prospects). That means your close rate is actually 20% out of 80%, which is 25%. If you drop the twenty non-responding prospects and add qualified ones instead, your 25% close rate will instead yield twenty-five customers a month!

Realize "no" does not mean "never." It just means "not now." Put this prospect back into the funnel for general marketing activities. Remember, the goal is not to sell them something now but to be there when they are ready to buy. A one-time initial purchase is not the ultimate goal, but rather, every company wants a long-time customer with a high lifetime value (LTV). When you add them to your monthly marketing funnel (as described in Chapter 11), contact them about the value you offer on a consistent basis. Eventually, if your product solves a pain they have (and they have the money), they will contact you. If they never contact you, then you never wasted time with someone who wasn't going to buy anyway.

CASE STUDY
LETTING YOUR FAVORITES GO
COMPUVOX

I had a bad habit of making sales calls to the same people over and over again. It was hard to break. I had traveled to go see a big corporation that had expressed interest in our new product. The demonstration could not have gone better. They had a need we could solve. All the right decision makers were there, and they had a budget for the project. At the end of the meeting, they told me to send a proposal. Back in the office the next day, I immediately sent them a letter and followed up by phone. I did not get a return phone call the next day. I kept calling every few days thinking they just had not received my message. I never heard from the company again.

To this day, I do not know what went wrong or why I never got a returned call from anyone in the company. What I do know is I wasted a lot of energy chasing and hoping this one corporation would call back. Strangely enough, once I stopped calling, with little effort, I found another major corporation to buy from me the following month. Letting go of that dead prospect enabled me to find a truly interested one.

CHAPTER 11

You Stop Marketing as Soon as Your Revenue Increases

WHY YOU ARE STUCK

You suffer from the "Double Helix Trap." Many times during the year, sales are booming. In other months, you are begging for business. You only market and actively sell your products when you have no revenue. As soon as you get customers again, you stop marketing. This happens because you need to be both the hunter (get the customers) and the gatherer (execute the work for the customers) in the company. This leaves no time, energy, or desire to direct an ongoing sales and marketing campaign.

You don't follow up on leads that are identified. After spending a lot of money identifying a new prospect, you only follow up with them once. If they don't buy at that time, their contact information gets relegated to the business card graveyard, which is located in a pile on your desk. Seventy-nine percent of marketing leads never convert into sales, according to Marketing Sherpa, and poor lead nurturing is the common cause of this weak performance rate.

HOW TO GET UNSTUCK

Learn the difference between selling and marketing. Most businesspeople say they hate to sell. This is not true. What people hate to do is market. Most businesspeople love selling to an identified prospect, once they know they can solve their problem. What they hate to do is find "suspects" and turn them into prospects. Suspects are targeted companies that have the problem your product or solution solves. For example, a vendor that sells customer relationship management (CRM) software (like Salesforce or Infusionsoft) might look for companies that need to keep track of and expand their customer contacts (people who have the problem they solve). Most companies of any size should be a suspect for them. But a "prospect" is a suspect that has "raised their hand" and said to the company in some way (like returning a phone call or email) that they have a need for CRM software. Those are the companies that have a higher probability to become your future customers.

This is exactly what marketing is all about. You need to constantly and consistently be marketing to your suspects, prospects, and current customers so you can be there for them when each of these groups is ready to buy. This is where the sales and marketing strategy of most high-growth companies fail. Most businesspeople spend their time marketing and selling to two types of companies. First, they sell to their current customers. This is a good target since conventional wisdom says it is a lot easier to get additional business from current customers than to find new ones. Also, it is an opportunity to turn these customers into evangelists and have them refer additional prospects. This is an important part of sales. There is nothing as powerful as a great referral from another client. As customer management consulting firm Peppers & Rogers calls it, you become the "trust agent." That means you get to bypass the building-credibility-and-credentials stage and go directly to, "When can you start?" This is the fastest way to build your business. The other set of businesses that, unfortunately, businesspeople spend a lot of time selling to is those past prospects that long ago stopped returning phone calls and emails, as discussed in the last chapter.

High-growth businesspeople need to spend much more time marketing to suspects and converting prospects into customers. These two groups are the future sales that will feed your pipeline. However, you need to market to these groups differently.

Suspect Marketing

Your suspect list is large. It consists of anyone whose business problems your company can solve. In most cases, the total universe is hundreds of thousands or millions of companies or individuals. Since it is not economical to directly sell to each suspect individually, the goal is to get him or her to somehow "raise their hands," as stated earlier. Following are five tactics for suspect marketing success:

1. **Advertise:** If you do not have a large budget, use trade journals or online publications where you can narrow the list of suspects for a reasonable amount of money. This will be a lot less expensive and a more targeted approach than general publications. Never advertise just once in a publication. To ensure you get maximum results, place as many ad insertions as you can in targeted publications at a size your budget can afford. More insertions at a smaller display size are better than a full page just once. Make every ad trackable so you can determine its return.

2. **Direct email:** Buy lists of "opt in" names from a broker, and use a marketing email system to track who opens the emails and who clicks through to your website. This may seem a bit sneaky, but today's technology allows you to do this. Suspects clicking through on your email is the equivalent of "raising their hands" so you can begin to get traction with each of them. Think about what the appropriate follow-up activity can be for each of these leads so they can be nurtured to a sale.

3. **Paid search:** Use Google AdWords or Yahoo!-Bing to promote your business on search pages. You only pay when a suspect clicks through to your website. The best part about paid search is that your company can set its own budget and even target a local area. You decide how high you want to be on the search list (by paying more) and how much money you want to spend each month. Note this is very difficult to effectively do alone. Depend on experienced interactive

marketing companies like Dex Media to help with an overall strategy.

4. **Trade shows:** If you have a large enough budget, pick a few targeted shows and exhibits. You may even want to mail a pre-show offer to attendees to incentivize them to come by your booth. If you are boot-strapping your business, it can be almost as effective to walk your industry trade show and collect cards from attendees. You could also try to participate on a conference panel to get increased exposure. Follow up with everyone you met by email and nurture these relationships as described above.

5. **Become an expert:** Write an article about something of value in your industry and get it published in print and online media. Companies buy from experts, and these external sources will give you additional credibility with suspects you do not know—they will act as "trust agents." You can also repurpose the article as content on your own website or a newsletter.

Prospect Marketing

Your prospect list is a dialed-down version of your suspect list. It is much smaller because the companies on this list fulfill three requirements: 1) You know they have a problem you can solve, 2) they have the money to solve the problem, and 3) you know the decision maker. In most cases, this universe will consist of 10 to 1,000 companies or individuals at any point in time, depending on the size of your company. You need to try to touch each of these prospects individually and as consistently as possible through a variety of media so you can be there at the moment when their pain is so great, they must buy something—and it might as well be from you! Following are four tactics to help you connect with these prospects:

1. **Direct sales:** Call and email your prospects to check the status of their pain or need and your solution to it. There is nothing wrong with be-

ing aggressive—just don't become annoying. What is the difference? Keep track of the last time you contacted them and when they called you. Don't call more than twice to every unanswered call from them. If these two calls aren't returned, you can call every few weeks for a month or so. No answer or reply? Then you no longer have a prospect, and you need to move on to other interested prospects.

2. **Referrals:** The right customer for you may not be the prospect themselves, but it may be someone they know. Stay in front of the prospect, and they will be thinking of you the next time an associate of theirs can use your services. As stated previously, this "trusted referral" is the most powerful sales tool in business. You can always ask for referrals at the right time. Maybe at a lunch you can say, "Do you know anyone else who my solution may help?" You will be surprised how helpful a satisfied customer can be!

3. **Direct email or postal mail:** This is a very cost-effective technique, since your numbers of prospects are limited. Send them industry information or articles of interest so they will continue to see you are the expert who can solve their problems. As with the other tactics, it's critical to become consistent at marketing. It is not something to do once or when you run out of prospects or your work dries up.

4. **Start to educate them.** Use a systematic marketing plan where your company brings expert value to prospects and customers on a monthly basis (not selling features). Before the Internet, experts said that a potential customer needed seven reinforcements of a brand until they remembered that company. Now, with the onslaught of inbound information targeting every customer, it takes twenty-one reinforcements. With no geographic boundaries and overnight shipping, every company that does what your business delivers is a competitor.

Customers buy from whom they know, like, and trust. It is critical to stay in contact with a potential customer so you are part of that "maybe pile" when a customer is ready to buy. This is not done by bombarding them with new product offers, discounted prices, or seasonal specials. Most prospects will ignore these offers if they do not have a current need. What the potential customer wants instead is value to solve problems they face every day. The internet may be filled with information, but even with great search engines like Yahoo!, Bing, and Google, it is still hard to find relevant information. This is where your company can highlight its brand by sending or mailing something of value to the prospect every month.

Here are some ideas:

- *Congratulate them on something or follow up on a significant event you know about that they just experienced.* This will show that prospect you are interested in them.

- *Are you both going to a particular trade conference?* Suggest that you both meet to connect in person.

- *Point out a recent article, tool, or book that was valuable to you.* This will demonstrate you are knowledgeable, and they can count on you for expert information.

- *Identify a resource or make a connection for them* to show that you want to help their business beyond just selling your products.

You know you need to stay in front of your customers, and you have some ideas on how to do that. Now you need to get them to open that email, and that starts with an intriguing title. Eighty percent of the reason someone opens an email is because of the title. Here are some examples:

- "Saw this and thought of you"
- "I know you appreciate a good resource"
- "I have an idea for you"
- "Here is a great connection for you"

Specific content examples for companies include:

HVAC: How to Keep Your Home More Energy Efficient

Garden Shop: When Is the Right Time to Plant Tulips?

Auto Repair: Will That Dent Rust?

Insurance Agent: Why You Need Long-Term Care

Plumber: The Biggest Danger in Your Home

The content needs to consist of single subjects, not a long complicated newsletter. With the flood of inbound information, prospects don't have time to read these, and companies have a difficult time assembling so much content in one place. Text should be no more than fifty words, with a single hyperlink to the additional content.

These touch points need to be done on a monthly basis. Don't get discouraged. It takes at least three months to form this habit. If there are 100 prospects or customers that need to be contacted, doing five a day will get you to the goal. Remember, promoting your brand with additional value should be a daily task—not something that just gets done when sales are lagging.

CASE STUDY

I FEEL LIKE I ALREADY KNOW YOU
KILLERSPIN TABLE TENNIS EQUIPMENT

Although I had never met Robert Blackwell Jr., I had worked with his father when I was at IBM more than twenty years ago. I had known of Blackwell for a long time as a very successful businessperson. Apparently, he had signed up for my weekly email newsletter many years ago. I had not realized this until he responded to one particular piece saying he would like us to have breakfast together.

When we met, the first thing that Blackwell said was "I feel like I already know you." Wow! This was the first time we had ever met in person; we had never even talked on the phone. Blackwell felt comfortable with me because he had been reading the weekly articles I had been sending for over a year. After that, when a pain came up in his business that he thought I could solve, he contacted me.

When prospects like, know, and trust you before they reach out for help, your chances of doing business together are extremely high.

CHAPTER 12
You Are Always Selling Product Features

WHY YOU ARE STUCK

You're selling like it's 1989. You sell your company's products based solely on its features. You believe people buy simply based on what the product does and its advantages over competitors. This is the way it was when I went through IBM sales training in the 1980s. We were taught to memorize all the features of a product so we could explain them to a customer. I even had to learn to write them upside down, as I sat across the desk from a prospect! At that time, people were exclusively looking to the salesperson to explain what the product or service did. There was no internet that today acts as a central source. Back then, the only reliable information about any products was directly from company representatives. How these were presented was also critical. As a result, most marketing and sales efforts were focused around memorized product features that were repeated to the prospects over and over again.

Your superior and fantastic features. As discussed in previous chapters, you think people buy a product because it's the fastest, cheapest, and most wonderful thing out there. You believe all you need to do is make them aware that it exists in the market, and they will run to buy it. This is why you have placed all your financial and emotional resources into product development and nothing is left for ongoing sales and marketing campaigns. You emphatically point to examples like Apple that successfully sell the best and most expensive solutions in the market. You conveniently forget about their billion-dollar marketing budget that goes along with those amazing products.[10]

HOW TO GET UNSTUCK

Sell the sizzle, not the steak. Features are the characteristics of a product or service. For example, a car's features might include the color of the paint, the size of the engine, the number of seats, or high gas mileage. It is important for customers to know about your features, but these alone won't convince a customer to buy them. In fact, customers consistently use only 20% of a product's features. Today, customers want to really know about a product's value. Think of it as the ways in which a customer's life will change positively because of your product. The benefits of owning a car might include independence or increased sex appeal. For many Americans, driving a particular car becomes an extension of how they feel about themselves. Customers may not care if the color of the car is green, but they do care that it makes them feel cool.

Educate, don't sell. In his book, *To Sell Is Human: The Surprising Truth About Moving Others*, Daniel H. Pink says sales is far from dead; rather, it is evolving. He insists that companies can be more successful if they focus on the act of persuading others rather than the standard technique of always working toward the close People no longer want to be sold products or services—they want to be educated about them. This is a huge distinction. With the Internet, prospects can do their own research on your products and its features before making contact with your company. They can find out what other people say about it and exactly what it is like to do business with you. Prospects have an increasing tendency to delete or disregard all the marketing messages they are bombarded with about your product's features and how wonderful it will be if only they buy it. Instead, as discussed in Chapter 11, use your branded marketing messages to educate them on how you and your product can help, instead of constantly spouting its features.

Build trusted relationships. People prefer to do business with people they trust. This is now being personified with companies. To build trust, every business needs to think about the value and expertise they bring to help customers solve their problems, not the products they can sell to them right now. Position your company as an expert in a certain area, and customers with that pain will come looking for you to buy solutions. A trusted relationship also increases that customer's lifetime value and profitability. It gives you the opportunity to expand their business horizontally or vertically to sell more types of products to the customer. For example, in 1994, Amazon started selling books. Once they established in the marketplace that they could reliably (meaning trustfully) deliver these books at a valuable price on time, they expanded to selling more types of consumer goods. I even bought my kayak on Amazon, which included free shipping! In the example in Chapter 1, if your company is known for selling lawnmowers, when they break, that customer will come back to you to see where they can get it fixed. Your business can then expand into repairing the products you sell (or provide a trusted referral to another company).

But don't rush the trust. Most small business owners are passionately impatient. They can't wait to go out and tell customers about their fantastic products. However, to establish trust first, it takes discipline not to sell anything at the start. When I visit a new prospective company, I never sell them anything in the first few contacts. I start by determining how I can help them. I know that if I do this, they will want to find ways to work with me. This process could take months or years.

Remember business relationships take more time to build than personal ones. Many companies don't have the patience to establish a relationship with a customer before they try to sell them something. John Jantsch, founder of Duct Tape Marketing, describes a systematic approach to building trustful relationships as a wheel with seven steps:

1. **Know:** Get to know whom the customer is and what problems they need to solve. Any research you do before approaching the customer

will always impress them. It will also enable you to ask better questions and find out what the customer really needs.

2. **Like:** The prospect hears good things about your company in the marketplace and from their peers. Monitor your online reputation to listen to what others are saying about your business. Thank supporters gracefully, and it will subtly encourage them to keep complimenting your company.

3. **Trust:** At the start, provide help at no fee so they begin to see your company as a source. At this stage, expect nothing in return. This does not mean giving away "the secret sauce" but rather "a taste" of the help you offer. Most customers do not expect something for nothing on a long-term basis.

4. **Try:** Let the customer try your product or service with no penalty. If they do not like it, they can return it. Consumer catalog company, Hammacher Schlemmer has a no-questions-asked return policy for the life of the product. Even though they sell at the highest price in the market, this policy encourages consumers to check out their unique products.

5. **Buy:** The customer makes the first real purchase once the first four steps are completed. This sale should be at profit since they see real value. A profit also ensures the company has the money to invest in the first four steps.

6. **Repeat:** The customer enjoys the product, so they buy it again and again. This is where the upfront investment becomes very profitable for the company, and the customer's lifetime value can increase exponentially.

7. **Refer:** The customer enjoys the product so much; they refer friends who may be interested in a purchase. This is the most powerful marketing anywhere because an unknown company with a referral can go from "who are you?" to "how can I buy?"

Reputation is the new marketing. According to the "Nielsen Global Trust Survey for Advertising Report," 92% of people trust recommendations from people they know. More important, consumers trust 70% of the opinions they read online from people they don't know. In their trust index, these results beat the trust levels that company-branded websites (58%) and online ads (33%) receive. In other words, reputation is more important than your company's brand or its direct paid advertising. Therefore, it is critical to pay attention to what people are saying about your company online. This can be as simple as responding respectfully to review sites like Yelp and TripAdvisor or tracking what people write on social media and online blogs. Use free tools such as Google Alerts or those available from Dex Media so you are alerted when a new review is posted.

While it may be tempting, never ignore the positive or negative comments customers write about your company. Rather, view it as a gift, since up to 90% of disgruntled customers will say nothing directly to the company. Instead, they will sulk away and never buy from that company again. However, they will continue to retell the story of their bad experience. I have retold the story of poor service at The Great American Bagel hundreds of times. When I ordered a dozen sliced bagels, they wanted to charge me five cents extra to slice each one. At the time, I did not express my outrage, but I have been retelling that story over and over again.

Remember that no news is not always good news. As previously stated, dissatisfied customers complain frequently but not directly to you. According to *Harvard Business Review*, 25% of customers are likely to say something positive about their customer service experience, but 65% are likely to speak negatively about it. In addition, 23% of customers who had a positive service interaction told ten or more people. However, 48% of customers who had negative experiences also told ten or more people.

So while customers are more likely to complain, see this as a positive opportunity. They have taken their valuable time to give feedback directly to your company (or via another channel). Then you get a chance to turn around their experience. Surveys show that dissatisfied customers whose problems are fixed become even more loyal to the company than if they never had difficulties at all. You also get valuable feedback that many other customers have likely experienced, but never mentioned. This has to be tracked on a continuing basis since customer service is a moving target and changes every month.

Listen, listen, and respond. Listen carefully to make sure you understand customers' concerns. Respond with empathy and vow to do better next time. Try not to find blame or hide problems that develop. Ask customers for their suggested solutions. Get back to them on how it will be resolved. Then collect all these concerns so an overall trend can be spotted within the company. You may not get a dissatisfied customer to buy again, but other prospects will see how the company handles issues when things go wrong. This will encourage them to take the risk of purchasing your product.

At Miraval Resort and Spa in Tucson, AZ, a customer's experience is always the top priority. As a result, it is extremely important to be aware of what people are saying about their brand online. It can mean the difference between gaining a new customer and losing one. Miraval monitors what their Internet and social media platforms mention daily. They are strategic about responding to every negative review about their resort since it can create a buzz. Miraval looks for constructive criticism and responds with empathy. They counter the negative content by building positive content in the form of video, blogs, and social media posts. This lifts favorable Google search results to the top. The negative links will then drift to the bottom of the page or move to the next page.

CASE STUDY
LEARN FROM WASTE
ORWAK

Customers are always more interested in what a product can do for them and less so in the product itself. Some companies have a great grasp of this concept, but none gets it quite like the large Norwegian-company, Orwak, which provides waste management services throughout Europe. It skillfully positions itself to be more than just a company that solves waste issues.

On its home page, Orwak lists all the benefits of its services in a succinct, effective bulleted format. It makes bold claims to encourage customers to consider its benefits. For example, "Orwak solutions achieve ten times less to give you ten times more in order to help you realize your waste management goals in the most profitable way."

Customers may ask what this statement really means. To answer their question, Orwak encourages customers to click on those bulleted benefits. When they do, they find out such things as "less transport means more money, less handling means more efficiency, and less energy means more savings." Orwak understands that customers can get waste management *elsewhere,* but they also know that customers really want to do things like save money and be efficient.

CHAPTER 13

You Are Selling a Product that can be Purchased Cheaper Elsewhere

WHY YOU ARE STUCK

"If you build it, they will come" is your mantra. You think that your product is unique, and as Kevin Costner said in the movie, *Field of Dreams*, "If you build it, they will come." Unfortunately, they don't arrive because your product has become a commodity without any real differentiating value. Customers can now buy a product they think is just like yours anywhere. This may be because the product is offered at a lower price or a more convenient time and place to make the purchase.

You think you have to be the lowest price. You believe the way to generate demand in the marketplace is to have the lowest prices. You think that you can steal customers from your competitors if you sell a similar product for less. You forget about the additional barriers to exit and the switching costs those customers will face. Unfortunately, as you lower your prices, competitors keep lowering their prices as well. It has now become increasingly difficult to have the lowest price and still make a profit for your company. You further justify those low-priced products, saying they are loss leaders in order to attract new customers, but you are now having a difficult time getting them to buy your more profitable products.

More products today are commodities. In the 1950s, containerized shipments started to eliminate geographic advantages. When any product could be shipped from one location to another, economically, in a short period of time, the entire world became one big geographic marketplace. With the Internet, customers can easily compare prices and buy from anyone in the world. If your product is really a commodity, it will only be purchased based on price. An example of a product that is now traditionally a commodity is office supplies. How can you tell if your company sells a commodity? Harvard Business School professor John Quelch says a signal is if the "speed from product launch to maturity is faster than ever before."

When you compete on price, you lose. Most small businesses can never afford to be the low-cost producer and, therefore, the lowest cost in the marketplace. With this strategy, gross margins increasingly shrink, and it can be the quickest way out of business. Bestselling business author and speaker Bob Burg says that the price winner can actually be the loser:

"Win the sale based on lowest price and you will most likely lose your customer the moment someone new comes along with an even lower price. If they buy from you on price, they'll also leave you based on price. If you go low enough, you won't have enough profit to keep your business sustainable. Plus, you'll be investing time, energy, and service into an account that doesn't pay for itself, keeping you from landing other, more profitable accounts. Or you might need to provide less service for accepting the low price, which will harm your customer, costing you in effectiveness and reputation . . . and ultimately, new business."

Low price isn't always the best deal. During the Great Recession, the "lowest price" business model became more popular with small businesses. There are two reasons why "low price" becomes a default marketing strategy. First, companies reason that it is simple supply-and-demand economics: The lower the price, the more customers will buy. Second, it encourages the business to be extremely efficient in order to remain profitable. However, the lowest price strategy isn't for everyone. In fact, it isn't for most businesses.

It is a lazy marketing strategy. Offering the lowest price is already an oversaturated business practice. Many businesses in a number of sectors are all furiously competing with one another to shave another dollar off the price of their products and are failing to distinguish themselves in any other way. As far as customers are concerned, there is no reason to choose one provider over another, apart from their pricing. If those businesses focused on other ways to provide value, such as service or building loyalty, then they would not appear so anonymous and actually have an easier time competing.[11]

HOW TO GET UNSTUCK

Stop pushing price; go for value. Focus instead on what value the customer will get by doing business with you. What pain will be alleviated? What will the financial return be as a result of the purchase? This can be accomplished more easily by targeting buyers who are at a much higher level in a company. Senior managers think of value and return on investment for the entire organization, but purchasing agents focus on getting the best price. This is because each of their job performances is evaluated on different metrics. Most employees and consumers are afraid to make the wrong decision, so they try to make the safe one or no decision at all. Ultimately, price is a very difficult metric to compete on unless your company is very large and sells many commodities. Superstores like Aldi or Office Depot can compete on price on popular items. However, part of their strategy is that once they get the consumer in the store or on their website, they will buy additional more profitable items. This is even the strategy behind those infamous door-busters on Black Friday, Cyber Monday, and Green Monday. Even Southwest Airlines, which is known for low prices, also competes on service and value. Even though they have a reputation as a discount airline, they consistently appear at the top of the airline satisfaction rankings every year.[12]

Respect "showrooming." This happens when a customer shops in one retail location (typically a physical one) and then checks on their smartphone to see if another company (like Amazon) carries the same product for less. In these cases, the very least that can be done is to sell it for a similar price. Recognizing how prevalent this trend is, Best Buy has a huge sign in front of their store declaring they will match any Amazon price. To combat "showrooming," give customers a reason to buy it in your store right now. Prices don't have to be the same, but they need to be similar (within 10%-20%). Make up this difference by having knowledgeable staff, a local flair, and follow-up service. Relationships are still easier to create in person than on the web. To determine what is right for your company, use a tool like Survey Monkey to conduct a two-question post-purchase email survey on why customers actually shop at your store. Questions should include:

- Why do you shop at our store (or on our website)?
- What do we do so well that you would recommend us to your friends and associates?

Design a new competitive advantage. I remember once judging a business plan competition, and I asked the entrepreneur what was their sustainable competitive advantage. They told me "Everyone else in my industry is stupid!" While I doubt this was true, most small business owners can't depend on this type of strategy. Instead, create a lasting competitive advantage with tactics like distribution, customers, intellectual property, and other value-added services. For example, these can include:

1. **Add in-store and on-site technology.** Use multimedia in your retail space by placing video displays throughout the store. This can be accomplished by positioning inexpensive tablets with headphones so customers can privately view demonstrations or listen to advice. For example, Scott Starbuck, at the Chicago retail store, City Soles, has tablets around his retail store to give more information about particu-

lar shoes. He turns the shoe shopping into an experience by telling the buyer the story of how and where they are made, about the designer, and what to wear them with. Another idea is to attach an informative video to every item on your website. Similarly, the education of the customer will be a value-add that can produce a higher purchase rate.

2. **Bundle with other products.** Quelch says, "Selling a commoditized product with differentiated ancillary services (such as after-sales service) can appeal to buyers willing to pay a premium for the convenience." When the customer has the opportunity to buy two products separately, bundling will raise the perceived value. For example, McDonalds offers an Extra Value Meal (burgers, fries, and a drink). Microsoft sells the MS Office product as a bundle of software including Word, Excel, and PowerPoint.

3. **Divide your market into segments.** Quelch says that large, mature markets may "be divided profitably into multiple segments. Marketers can focus on providing specific product or industry expertise for less price-sensitive customer segments for which the product is still important." For example, in a recent report on market segmentation for TRC Consumer Insights, Maynard Robison explains that banks traditionally segment their customers since a checking account is seen as a commodity. Many offer different services to each segment: the "committed," the "active," and the "parkers." The "committed" stay with the bank no matter what happens. Rates or products do not affect their choices. The "active" use many of the services the bank has to offer. The "parker" deposits money and has few transactions with the bank.

4. **Train your staff again and again.** Studies show the reason many customers shop at a store is to get advice from their staff. More knowledge means better customer service and increased sales. Many companies use internal quizzes and mystery shoppers to test their employees.

Empower them to make decisions for your customers 95% of the time. It is also important for you as the owner to work in the store alongside your employees. This improves their training and raises their performance level.

5. **Showcase popular brands.** Tie recognizable national brands to your own store, and use them to influence the emotional decisions customers make when purchasing your products. By positioning your brand on top of theirs, you take advantage of all their advertising. For example, a music store can showcase Fender or Gibson guitars to attract customers.

6. **Use mobile point of sale (POS) applications.** Equip staff with smartphones that can be used to check out customers on the spot instead of lining up at a traditional register. This will strengthen the connection between shopping and actual purchasing since the salesperson can ask for the order. Apple was one of the first retailers to use this effectively.

7. **Really go mobile.** This is becoming more critical to online success, since 50% of all searches are mobile, and 70% of those searches end in a purchase. Unfortunately, 90% of small business' websites don't show up easily on mobile devices. Fix this by having a mobile website that displays easily on smartphones and tablets. The site should be customized with mobile menus so it can be searched without magnifying the screen. Test these often as new devices and formats are introduced to the market.

8. **Offer a no hassle return policy.** Many retailers are reluctant to offer a return policy on products that can't be resold. However, show confidence in your products so the consumer can shop with less fear. Understand the lifetime value of a customer, and do not focus just on a single purchase. While you don't have to offer a lifetime guarantee like Hammacher Schlemmer, do give customers the opportunity to use your product. Ensure that your policy is specific and applied

uniformly across all customers. For example, it is now traditional for retailers to pay returned shipping.

9. **Keep your customer influence.** Contact customers monthly, even when they don't visit your website or store. This can be easily accomplished through email marketing as discussed in Chapter 11. This is critical since companies lose 10% of their influence on customers with every month they do not reinforce their brand.

CASE STUDY

GETTING TO KNOW YOUR BURGER PERSONALLY

JACK IN THE BOX

East of the Rocky Mountains, the world of fast food is dominated by the likes of Wendy's, Burger King, Hardees, and McDonalds. However, when you explore the West and Southwest, you'll come across a rather different fast-food chain known as Jack in the Box. Jack in the Box does not distinguish itself in terms of its menu (it's typical fast-food fare of burgers and fries) but rather by its distinct marketing and social media personality. Jack in the Box cultivates and carefully preserves a special reputation of being a fast-food company that refuses to take itself, its food, or even its customers very seriously, and it does this through continuous social media management.

Jack in the Box mostly works through Facebook, Twitter, and YouTube. The company boasts nearly 900,000 "likes" on Facebook, and its commercials are shown on YouTube to some 3,200 subscribers and hundreds of thousands of viewers. Jack in the Box carries a simple message to its customers through its social media: "You are hungry; we can feed you." The company mascot, Jack, is a wisecracking puppet that cheerfully informs his customers about his restaurant's new products with plenty of sass. Jack in the Box does not bother with justifying its food as being anything other than delicious, satisfying, and affordable. This refreshing honesty makes the company seem like more than a business, and Jack seems like a friend.

The best social media campaigns encourage customers to engage freely and happily with other customers and with the company itself. Jack in the Box does an exceptional job of doing this with their amusing video commercials, irreverent and savvy social media posts, and their overall branding as a restaurant chain unafraid to tell it like it is.

CHAPTER 14

You Go On Social Media Sites without a Strategy

WHY YOU ARE STUCK

You think you don't need one. In your opinion, unless you are selling products to Generation Y customers, you don't have a business need for social media. It's just a fad you don't have the time for. Besides, when you do surf Facebook or Pinterest, you want to keep it fun and a personal distraction. You see it as the modern-day smoke break (maybe even as unhealthy). Recently, you have become more interested in gossip than helping business prospects. Any type of marketing strategy around social media would make it too serious and take all the excitement out of it.

You think the purpose of social media is to sell your products. It's just a digital billboard. You use social media to post special pricing or to announce new product arrivals. It is simply another form of your product advertising, especially for events like Cyber Monday. You are constantly asking people to buy on these sites without getting to know who they really are or what they are interested in.

You are talking at people, not with them. You are not having two-way conversations with anyone online, but you are continually broadcasting your own company message. Think of this when you go to a party and the conversation you are having really turns into a monologue for you to listen to. How interested are you in what that person is saying? Online, a good indication of this is when no one ever responds to your posts (and you are left wondering why).

You are talking to the wrong people. Because you have no strategy for your social media efforts, you talk to anyone who will talk to you. This is because you may have outsourced it to a random Gen Y-er, instead of someone with specific digital channel experience who can target your customers and prospects.

You ask others to retweet or share your content but never talk to them any other time. The only time you communicate with social media partners is to ask them to share your stuff. For example, you send this type of message: *"Good morning! Hey would you be willing to send a tweet for me if I wrote it and DM'd it to you?"* Many times, you get a "no" reply or a "will do," but you never see the post.

You broadcast the same message across all channels. You use a social media tool like HootSuite to make it easy to broadcast the exact same message across all the social media sites, even though people communicate differently on each one of them. You think what is important is the quantity of posts, not the quality. For example, you think people on Facebook won't care if there is a hashtag in the post and no picture.

You focus on numbers, not the quality of people. You are obsessed with the number of followers instead of the quality of their interaction with your company. You celebrate when you have a new follower regardless of who it is. You "friend" and "follow" dozens of people each day, with the only goal that they will follow you back.

You post infrequently or irregularly. No one knows when you will show up on social media or post new content. You are so busy with other tasks at your company that you post approximately once a week at different times. You have no schedule or content guide for blog posts and only produce the occasional random YouTube video.

You neglect posting the same things multiple times during the day or week. You post when you think of it or have a spare moment, instead of scheduling it using a professional tool.

You do not monitor what people are saying about your company. You would rather ignore it than face any comments, since you already deal with enough customer issues.

You delete negative comments. Your solution to those angry customers is to delete their negative comments on social sites or simply not respond. You hope they just go away or no one reads them. You hope the positive comments outweigh the negative ones.

You have no employee social media policy. Employees wonder if it is acceptable to check their social media status updates at work. They also don't know if they can post on behalf of the company. Everyone does something different.

You use photos and videos that do not reflect your company. You use your company logo instead of something that better represents the values behind your brand. The only video posted is a short clip from a recent company party. It is difficult to find any pictures or videos of your company, its products, or customers anywhere on the web.

You send automated direct messages to followers on Twitter. You know that it is not very personal. However, it is more convenient and efficient this way because it is difficult to keep up with all your new followers. You reason that "something" is better than "nothing."

You use too many hashtags. With every tweet or Facebook post, you insert a #newhashtag, even if no one else has ever used that hashtag.

HOW TO GET UNSTUCK

Use social media as just an additional marketing tool. Map out how your company will use this marketing tool and how results will be measured. Listen first, listen some more, and then talk later. Find out where customers are talking about the pain your company solves. Offer help first without selling your products or services. For example, think about when you meet people for the first time at a dinner party. Would you try to sell them your product in the first conversation? When in doubt, follow that model.

Engage in two-way conversations. It's called social for a reason. Marketing now is not a one-way message, but rather something more interactive. Customers no longer want to be talked at, but talked with. Get off the balcony and come down into the crowd. Don't ask people on social media to share your posts. If it is compelling content, they will share it spontaneously. Your reposting of other people's information should be 80% of all your social interactions. If it is absolutely critical that someone shares your post, you should always ask how you can help them first before asking for yourself.

Follow the right people. It is very difficult to monitor individual social media posts from anyone's main activity stream. Create a list of current customers and a second list of prospects. Set up these lists in Twitter and Facebook so you can monitor and respond when these people post. This is a critical step in creating relationships. For example, set up a private list on Twitter for top customers that are active with that tool. A good way to get more prospects is to look at specific problem-oriented hashtags and track who participates in those conversations. Some people may already have built their own list of those people, and you can follow that one as a shortcut if it is public. On Facebook, set up a special-interest group for all your prospects in a specific vertical industry.

Stop broadcasting the same message across all the channels. Gary Vaynerchuk reminds readers in his book, *Jab, Jab, Jab, Right Hook* that to maximize their social media effectiveness, all companies need to tailor their message for each specific channel. For example, Twitter needs to be a short and informative statement with a link for more information. A Facebook post always should include a picture. A Pinterest post should have a more stylized photograph. On LinkedIn, it should be much more business-tip-oriented without a picture.

Size does not matter. Stop being obsessed with the sheer number of followers. Instead, focus on who those followers are and how your company interacts with them. This marketing channel is not a numbers game, but one where the depth of the relationship is what counts. Think about the value of each new follower, not the number of followers that you want to gain. One hundred dedicated followers will spread your message much more effectively than 10,000 followers who never interact with your company.

Post regularly. Have a regular schedule to show dependability and consistency of your message. For most companies, this should be at a minimum once per day. Post the same items multiple times during the day or week since people are not on all at the same time. Most social media posts have a short shelf life. For example, the average Twitter post is only seen for fifteen minutes. For Facebook, it may be a few hours, and on LinkedIn, it may be up to a day. Tools such as Social Oomph can be used to schedule posts in advance. However, these automated posts need to be monitored. If a significant world event happens, and you are the only one posting about how to purify water, it will detract from your marketing efforts.

Listen: They are talking about you. As discussed in Chapter 12, reputation is your biggest marketing weapon. Customers now place more trust in online reviews by customers than company advertisements. You need to know what everyone is saying about you. Set up Google Alerts or use tools from Dex Media. Use keywords that list the key areas you cover: competitors, customers, and important prospects.

Institute a social media policy. During breaks, allow employees to check their social media statuses and have their own "handles." They will do it anyway, so you should not make it a point of conflict. However, make it clear that it should not interfere with their jobs (See Chapter 14). Their profiles should mention the company, but state that their views are their own. Employees are one of the most authentic ways to spread the company's mission and culture. With all the places they visit online, they are a good resource to keep track of what is being said about the company.

Say it in pictures. Use photos beyond your logo on social media sites. As discussed, brands evoke the passions customers use to buy your product. Think about what your pictures and videos say about your company. Every company should have pictures or video of their employees, since it makes the business human. There should also be pictures or video of customers using your products. FAQ videos are especially useful if you sell a physical product or a computer application.

Respond to every comment. As discussed in Chapter 12, use empathy and understanding. This is what customers really want. Not responding is an admission by the company that the business does not care about what their customers think. Multiple unanswered negative comments will reinforce the perception that dissatisfied customers are right.

Stop sending automated direct messages to followers on Twitter or Facebook. This is the equivalent of email and text spamming. Only send direct messages that are customized for whom you want to connect with. If your company does not have the resources to accomplish this, don't use the feature.

Stop using hashtags for every post. Use them to be included in an overall conversation or subject matter, not to emotionally highlight the subject of the post. If other users do not actually post with that hashtag, it is meaningless. Hashtags are a great way to get involved in the discussion of a particular conversation and to engage customers and prospects on that subject. Unfortunately, #WhyYourBizIsStuck has no posts (so far!).

CASE STUDY

Toffee with a Side of Warmth and Nostalgia

Ella Riley's Toffee

Ella Riley's Toffee, a small confectionary in South Wales, was once a staple business for locals, providing delicious toffee and other sweets for many years. The confectionary was shut down for some time, but then in 2009, the company was reopened to the delight of the locals. The company has since become more successful than ever and is considering franchising. This success was made possible by its strong and genuine social media campaign.

Freya Sykes, co-owner of Ella Riley's Toffee, says that her social media campaign has focused on creating "a feeling of warmth and nostalgia." The company communicates through its social media channels continuously and hits emotional buttons, such as the smell of hot toffee, the warm building on a cold winter's day, and other such descriptive language.

Sykes uses different platforms for various purposes. Facebook is used primarily to engage customers about their experiences with the business, their memories of the products, or to alert followers about special events or new products. Twitter is used for defending the brand and the company's patent on toffee, using a hashtag campaign called "#realrileys" to alert people about counterfeit businesses. Pinterest showcases past and present products and gives customers a good look at the delicious candies and the facilities.

Sykes says that with social media, "You can talk to customers in a tone of voice that you can't get with an advert."

CHAPTER 15

You Hate Your Customers
(and Maybe Even Your Employees or Vendors)

WHY YOU ARE STUCK

It's hard to admit, but you really hate your customers. You think they are whiners and always impossible to please. No matter what you offer, they always seem to want more. Come to think of it, this is exactly the way you feel about your employees and vendors. You know you're the boss and it's your company. Doesn't this entitle you to do whatever you want? Why don't they all listen to you? Why aren't they satisfied with what you offer them? There are times you feel that your personal loyalty has been betrayed. You have noticed lately that your employees are starting to act like you and complain about the same dissatisfaction with customers, vendors, and each other. As a result, sometimes you dream that a perfect business would be one without customers or employees!

You never meet with people in person. It has become much more comfortable to sit in your office or at home and talk via email, phone, or chat. You rarely meet people face to face since it has become messy. It's too much effort and an inefficient use of your valuable time. You think you can get more done not being with other people. In fact, you have not seen many of the employees for years that work remotely.

You are always searching. You lack real loyalty to your employees, vendors, and customers. You are always looking for a customer that will pay you more money for a higher profit or who is easier to deal with. You want employees who will work longer hours and make less money. You seek vendors that will offer lower prices and longer payment terms each year.

You never want to pay the best people the most money. You always hire young people at entry wages and get disappointed when they don't perform to your high expectations. You understand that more experienced people cost more but can't seem to justify the short-term investment. You are always looking for a deal, even when it comes to employees.

You confuse recognition with rewards. You hand out cash rewards for what you think are great performances. You don't understand why this subjective method of recognizing employees never seems to motivate any of them to do a consistently better job.

HOW TO GET UNSTUCK

Stop searching first. While there may be more ideal customers, employees, or vendors out there, it is impossible to look for them all at the same time. If you are dissatisfied with all of them simultaneously, then you may be in the wrong business. Instead, prioritize the needs of your business by area. If the customers currently are contributing to a profitable business, stop complaining about them. Weed out the few that are real problems or are unprofitable for the business. If current employees do not have the skills to accomplish today's job (or the near future's), then begin to look for replacements. If there are particular employees who are poisoning the company culture, they need to be let go immediately, regardless of what they contribute. Do deals with current vendors allow your company to make a large enough profit margin to produce a healthy bottom line? If not, this should be high on your priority list.

Get interested now. To build a business, you must be sincerely interested in your customers', employees', and vendor's success. Here's how:

- **For employees:** Find out what their career goals are in working at the company and where there is common ground. Employees stay and excel at a business only when these two goals are aligned.

They quit when these do not match. Practice this golden rule by treating all of them the way you would want to be treated. Build a supportive company culture for their career aspirations, and they will work hard for your business over a sustained period of time.

- **For customers:** Find out why they really buy your product or service. What pain does it solve for them, and what is its value? Explore why they think about doing business with your company. This must include the good, the bad, and the truly ugly. Listen to their concerns, take action, and give feedback.

- **For vendors:** Find out what their individual business goals are. How important of a customer are you to them? Where are your common goals? Find out how both companies make a profit together. Identify where your objectives compete. Brainstorm on how this gap can be bridged.

Go out and meet people in person. Technology has made a lot of businesspeople lazy. We think we no longer need to go out and see people in person to create relationships. This is dead wrong. The best way to build and grow relationships is still in person. Force yourself to spend focused time with employees, customers, and vendors on a weekly basis. You will learn and build things from this activity that you never could sitting behind your desk.

Build a culture of like. All your negativity around customers and vendors builds a culture of dislike and dissatisfaction within your company. It is a cancer that spreads. This may first be evident by the negative tone of how employees disparage customers over email, chat, or in person. It grows into an "us against the customers" (or the world) mentality. This type of negative energy is not part of building a winning culture. It's very easy to pay lip service to customer satisfaction. After all, no companies publicly advertise, "We hate our customers and want nothing to do with them." But it's actually frightfully easy to create a company culture that seems to be apathetic, or even hostile, toward its customers. To be successful, you must truly have a passion for helping your customers and not see them as the enemy. Remember, they pay you money to solve their pain, so do not be surprised if they come to you with it.

Build a Company Culture That Truly Loves Its Customers

Accomplishing this is not difficult, and it's not too late to change course. Here's how.

Hire employees who believe in your values. Despite what many people think, most employees are not mercenaries who are out looking for the best paycheck. Most people are interested in doing meaningful work for a company they can believe in. Develop clear values for your company, stand by them, and hire employees who agree with them. That way, they will interact well with your customers, who will also be aligned with your values. When you treat your employees well, they will treat your customers even better.

Don't just create an office. Create a community. If your employees are constantly working together to solve problems, they will be more inclined to be supportive and collaborative with customers. Have weekly events for employees, employ social media to communicate outside the office, and organize community resources such as carpooling or coffee runs.

Create measurable goals and criteria. Employees will be far more likely to love their customers if they know how to love them. Train your employees in customer service techniques, empower them to make decisions that help customers (even if they have to bend other rules to make it happen), and give them clear goals for customer satisfaction when possible.

Start giving recognition, not just rewards. According to brand-integrity expert and author Gregg Lederman, giving financial rewards is not the same as recognizing outstanding employee performances. Many small business owners think the formula for getting peak performance from their employees is simple: Tie their pay or other cash rewards directly to narrowly defined performance goals. Here is why this never works to get the desired results:

- **It's shortsighted.** Giving a reward may provide a short-term boost to achieve a specific target, but employees then have the tendency to ignore the rest of their job (and the majority of the reason they are getting paid) in order to get the next bonus. A study by incentive travel company World Incentives found that "50% of employees who receive cash awards either did not remember what they used the money for or used it to pay down credit card debt."

- **Many goals simply can't be defined objectively.** Not everything can be tied to a number. Many small business owners try to put every goal into a complicated numerical formula, but this only serves to confuse employees and, ultimately, motivates no one. Alternately, if achieving the goal is subjective, it becomes less of a motivator since the employee will think the manager will not give out awards fairly. As a result, they stop striving for it.

- **The top motivator is not money.** Many studies show that in the list of what motivates people; money never comes out on top. A study published last year by German and Swiss researchers found that gifts were far more motivating to employees than cash bonuses on improving productivity.[13] This experiment showed the thought and effort of bosses mattered more than the actual incentive. In the study, cash was simply sent in an envelope to some employees. To others, it was delivered as "a five-Euro note folded into an origami shirt and a two-Euro coin with a smiley face painted on it." The origami money-gift generated the highest increase in productivity by employees.[14]

- **Employees will always "game" the program.** Some team members will always figure out a way to go around or go under the rules. They will spend a lot of time trying to fix the odds in their favor. They will focus on the prize and not the work required to get it or the value of achieving the goal.

So what do you do instead?

- **Pay above-industry salaries.** While this can be difficult to accept for many small business owners just trying to get by, well-paid employees will brag to others, and it will serve as "golden handcuffs" for them to stay at the company. People realize that they are making more than their peers are and will work hard to earn their compensation and stay on the team. Having a reputation that you pay employees well will mean a lot to your customers too. When I left IBM, my new boss paid me $20,000 more than I was earning. This "bought" a lot of dedication.

- **Give timely praise or attention**. As business management Guru Ken Blanchard says, mangers are more effective when they "catch an employee doing something right." Give feedback in a very timely fashion and address employee suggestions or concerns each week. Remember that only giving an annual review is a management relic from the past.

- **Give employees a voice in making decisions.** Most people do not want to be told how to do something but instead want influence in deciding how it gets done. When they have a chance to exercise their own judgment, they will be happier and ultimately more successful.

- **Create a community.** Employees want to feel like they are part of something bigger than themselves. They will work harder toward collective goals. Most people are actually happiest when they sacrifice for others to achieve a higher mission.

CASE STUDY
LOVE MAKES THE CORPORATION GO 'ROUND
CORREDERA CORPORATION*

They would never admit it, but almost every employee at Corredera Corp. hated their customers. I was never sure if they really hated them, but all their communication with them and among employees showed they really disliked them. In emails and chat, they referred to customers as jerks, morons, and idiots. While Corredera had built a profitable business over ten years, all the managers had to work very hard every day to make it successful. Since their value proposition was doing great work in a very short period of time, customers always demanded more and more results (and wanted to pay less) for their top dollar. They always exceeded customer expectations, but it was getting harder to achieve the same results. This put a lot of stress on the company culture, which became one of negativity and anger. The company began to realize this attitude was holding them back.

Corredera was finally able to revise its culture by refocusing its brand on products that were not time-based, but could instead be delivered whenever customers needed them. Its shrink-wrapped products took the time pressure off delivery. The company also fired the 10% of its customers that were truly abusive. Once the managers and employees were able to truly love and care about their customers, they not only sold more but also were able to retain their employees.

Fictional company

CHAPTER 16

You Only Hire Employees Who Are Weaker Than You

WHY YOU ARE STUCK

You are afraid of people knowing more than you. You like being *the* only expert. Ironically, it's not enough just to be the boss and the owner. You need to know more than anyone else about everything so you can have daily control. This applies to knowledge about your industry, customers, vendors, and all the inner workings of the company. As a result, you only hire weaker "B" players who will be happy to work in supporting roles. Predictably, your "B" employees do a poor job by hiring "C" players who mimic your hiring pattern. You continue to wonder why your organization starts to crumble from the top down. You have failed to achieve exactly what you need to grow a business: leverage. You are unable to use other people's skills since they are so weak. You remain "all powerful" while the company remains unable to grow. As discussed in Chapter 4, you still have "the monkey on your back" and can't confidently delegate any of the important company decisions. In fact, you need to keep track of every major endeavor so it remains on track.

You are the center of the universe. You continue to use a hub-and-spoke organization where all-important decisions must come through you. While the official organization chart is hierarchical, the only real power center is you. Your employees constantly lining up in front of your office to ask your opinion on even the most fundamental business issues demonstrate this. In fact, they look to you in all decisions so they do not have to take responsibility. By making decisions for them, they don't have to make their own since they know, somewhere along the way, you will jump in and do their job. It makes you feel important that you monitor everything inside your company. This keeps you incredibly busy, with little time to accomplish your own tasks.

You are always invoking emergency powers. You have officially delegated decision-making to your managers, except in critical situations. This has become boring for you. So more and more, everything inside the company becomes an emergency situation. You are increasingly jumping into every business decision to direct what will happen. You then wonder why even in noncritical issues, employees come to you for decisions.

You have a fragile ego. You are afraid of anyone making you look bad in front of your peers, employees, vendors, or customers. Your self-worth is totally wrapped around the company, and you do not want it challenged. You are unsure if it is better to be liked or feared. Perhaps your family situation is unstable, so you work to make the company your complete domain. I worked for a small business owner like this. He wanted to find out why his salespeople were failing to close deals, since he had been so skilled at this part of the business. In interviews with his employees and customers, I discovered that no sale happened where there wasn't some type of big issue that erupted at the last minute. It seemed that the owner would privately sabotage key sales situations so he could come in later and save them to be the hero. When I reported my findings to him, he fired me. I found out later that his salespeople had a tendency to stay at the company because they could earn large commissions and have the owner do all their work.

HOW TO GET UNSTUCK

Change the math. As an "A" type of player, when you hire only "B" players, the math is not in your favor. This creates a company that gets weaker as it moves down the organization chart and away from you. If an "A" player is 90% effective, a "B" player is 70% effective, and both are involved in decision-making, the result will be 63% successful. Add the "C" player into the mix, who is 50% effective, and the result will be 32% successful. Alternately, if three "A" players work together, they will be 73% successful. Which organization would you like to be a part of?

Hire employees better than you. This is how you need to change your hiring mind-set. The best situation is to get team members who have complementary skills in areas where you are weak or disinterested. For example, if you love product development, find someone who can do all the office management. Ultimately, you need to find joy (and relief) that there are people in your company who can do a job better than you. Remember, this is what you are paying for as an employer. It is a tough realization for any small business owner when they finally discover they can no longer do every job in the company. In my last business, I was especially disappointed when I no longer had time to open the company mail. In these pre-e-mail days, this was the central hub of all business communications where I could monitor everything. As discussed in Chapter 15, stretch your budget to hire the best people you can afford. Get people who will challenge your point of view, if that's what it takes, to find an ideal business solution. Until you hire people better than you, the company will never have the ideas and energy (i.e., leverage) to expand the way that it needs to in order to be successful.

Check your ego at the door. Strangely enough, "Ego, the Living Planet," was a Marvel comic book character created in 1966 as the enemy of Thor. His origin is described as:

"Like all celestial bodies, Ego evolved from gas and dust to become a planet. For some inexplicable reason, however, this particular planet achieved sentience and the ability to move of its own volition. Like all living organisms, Ego needs to consume matter to survive, and began absorbing space vessels and even other worlds. Ego is exceptionally intelligent . . . it suffers from a God complex and can be emotional if thwarted." [15]

Sound familiar? Many small business owners "consume" employees, customers, and vendors to survive. This is one reason that turnover is so big. Daily business news offers examples of how leaders' egos become too large and central to their businesses. In many cases, it forced the downfall of their companies and, in some instances, jail time. It's easy to understand how successful companies become personified by their customers. It is much more comfortable to buy from a person instead of an entire corporation. As a result, the passionate leader becomes the brand, and customers relate to the confidence this person demonstrates in their company's products or services. When customers think Microsoft, they see Bill Gates more than they see Steve Ballmer. Although he passed away, Apple is still Steve Jobs, not Tim Cook. Richard Branson is still Virgin Brands, and Yahoo! has become Marissa Mayer. Every major sports team in the world selects a player to be the advertising "face of the team" for that year. For example, Derrick Rose is currently the face of the Chicago Bulls basketball team.

But a small business owner's passion, unchecked ego, and the belief that they are right in everything they do causes them to sometimes stay the course. With this "Midas touch" (as described in Chapter 2), they use their own ego to gain the controlling hand among those in their company who seek to challenge their authority on every disagreement. An ego can be a powerful management tool, but controlling yours, no matter how strong, is critical to empowering employees to get the job done themselves. Not making the decision for them is the only method of truly holding them accountable for the results. Do not always express your opinion on how something should be done (or do it last). Implement someone else's solution and make them responsible for completing it. Build up other deserving employees' self-confidence through a series of appropriate long-term rewards (See Chapter 15). When outstanding people are hired, and you make room for their egos, they will fill that void.

Let other people be the hub. Implement a hierarchical decision-making process so actions can move forward without you. Your ability to get things done in a larger organization relies on hiring managers who are more skilled than you. As a business owner, this is the only way to get the leverage you need to succeed. Letting go of total control is probably one of the most difficult transitions a business founder needs to make. When a company starts out, the organization looks like this—just one dot, the founder. As the company grows, the hub-and-spoke organization becomes a series of dots all clustered around and reporting to the founder. True successful leverage and growth in an organization happens when the founder is able to grow the confidence to trust other managers in the company. Ultimately, as the company expands, you can't be everywhere, and unless you hire strong "A" players, success will not follow.

Practice the two-step. Letting go of all tasks at once is not the solution. From total control to no-control can send panic through even the best owner. Instead, use a two-step process to start giving one strategic task to your best person to complete. Help set the goal, how it will be achieved, what success will look like, and its due date for completion. Monitor the ongoing results. When this is successful, delegate more tasks to the same person, but this time have them determine how it will be achieved. As things progress, include other employees in a similar two-step process. Retain a meticulous process of review. Remember, people respect what you inspect.

CASE STUDY
GIVING UP CONTROL
FINDING YOUR PEARL*

Marie Pearlstein (not her real name) ran a small, profitable company for many years. Her success revolved around having a focused business with a few highly skilled customer service people. When her growth started to explode, Pearlstein found that she needed to hire a team to help manage the twenty employees that were directly reporting to her. At first, she promoted her best people to these management positions, but they had a difficult time breaking the mold of having her make all the decisions. It was also difficult for other employees in the organization to go to their new manager instead of Pearlstein. The second step was to hire inexperienced managers from the outside to take over part of the business. This ended in disaster because they did not know the industry and did not have a true track record of managing a team. Pearlstein ended up doing their jobs—and all the employees knew it. Finally, she invested her profits in hiring one top-level executive from a major competitor for product development. This was the area where she was particularly weak. When this was successful, Pearlstein hired a controller to handle all the finance, office, and technology. The final piece was recruiting a sales and marketing executive who completed her management team. Over the last five years, the company has grown from $3 million to $20 million in sales—all because Pearlstein was willing to cease control and give it to others who were better than her.

Fictional company

CHAPTER 17

You Allow Lousy Employees (and Customers) to Overstay Their Welcome

WHY YOU ARE STUCK

You don't fire employees who are underperforming, even though everyone in the company knows they are doing a bad job and it hurts the company's morale and profit. You complain to your spouse or friends about them, but you can't seem to face firing them because you can't admit you made a mistake. Firing them would expose your mistake to the entire company or might show your lack of loyalty. It is always difficult to fire anyone, especially in an economy with high unemployment, and when you personally know the family they need to support. You also fear legal or organizational repercussions that would be harmful to the bottom line. The fired employee may take legal action against the company. Or after the employee is let go, you worry others will follow. You finally reason that the employee you know is better than the new employee you don't know and end up doing nothing at all.

You let misbehaving employees run the show. There are high-performing people who consistently disregard company policies and openly defy your instructions. There seems to be a different set of rules for them than other employees. They run counter to your culture, mission, and values. Other employees are starting to mention them by name when they decide not to follow a certain company policy. You are afraid of firing them because you might lose customers in the process or their knowledge of the job. Your biggest fear is that no one at the company is trained to take over their position.

You let destructive and unprofitable customers stay. There are some large customers you suspect are unprofitable for your company, but you keep doing business with them. What's worse, they are abusive to your employees, which hurts morale. These are the companies that everyone makes fun of around the water cooler and in company meetings. Being a small business, you think you need to keep every customer, regardless of their profitability or whether they support your company's values. You reason that this is the price of doing business and counsel your team to suck it up.

You stick with unreliable vendors. These companies never get the product needed when they promised for the contracted price. Their services always run over budget, overtime, and under quality. In turn, your customers are becoming increasingly unhappy with your business. You don't want to switch vendors because of all the work it takes to research and establish a new vendor relationship. You reason that the devil you know is better than the devil you don't.

HOW TO GET UNSTUCK

Fire nonperformers or destructive employees now. Excellent performing employees are a critical success factor in building a profitable business. But employees who don't follow the rules or support the company culture are a liability, not an asset. Effectively firing poorly performing employees is a very important, yet sensitive process. So what do small business owners do when they have a star employee who is volatile and destructive to their company?

Marketing expert Seth Godin characterizes these people as vampires:

"These are people that feed on negativity, on shooting down ideas, and most of all, on extinguishing your desire to make things better. Vampires cannot be cured. They cannot be taught. And they cannot learn the error of their

ways. Most of all, vampires will never understand how much damage they're doing to you and your work. Don't buy into the false expectation that in an organizational democracy, every voice matters. Every voice doesn't matter—only the voices that move your idea forward, that make it better, that make you better, that make it more likely you will ship work that benefits your tribe."

The sooner business owners come to a realization, the quicker their companies can move forward. Although it may be hard to understand, in this case, these businesses can actually grow by subtracting people. Only keep employees whose personal career objectives match the company's goals. Once their objectives deviate from what the company needs to be successful, it is time to part ways. In many situations, this may actually be beneficial for both parties. There were a few times when I was fired and I was more relieved than upset when it was all over.

Follow the "Cringe Factor." This is a simple method to determine who should be fired first. Ask yourself these questions: Which employees make me cringe every time I sign their payroll check? And if this employee got hit by a bus, how would it affect the company? If the answer is "none" or "I would pay the bus driver to do it," you have identified an employee to fire. Additionally, if your spouse or family knows these poor-performing employees by name because of your constant complaining, this is also a clue. Ask yourself, Why are they still with the company? Remember profit is the reason you are in business, and any nonperforming or problem employee subtracts from that equation.

Aim, function, fire. Any employee firing should be done on your timetable, not theirs. Make sure you have a description of everything that person does and the skills it takes to accomplish those tasks. Identify who within the organization can take over these tasks, or hire a person to replace them, even if only on an interim basis. This is also a good time to determine why certain people are doing given jobs and if that task distribution is still effective.

Provide an escort. No one likes to fire an employee because it can be physically debilitating. Do it quickly with another manager present first thing in the morning. Offer few explanations that can legally come back later to haunt you. Offer a week's severance for every year of service. Immediately turn off their computer access to company systems and gently escort them out of the office. Nothing can be accomplished by having them stay for additional days. Announce to the entire staff simultaneously, without an explanation of the termination that can get you into trouble later.

Don't skip the 28-day check. In many states, a company is responsible for unemployment benefits for an employee thirty days after hiring them. The more employees you fire, the higher your unemployment insurance rate rises. This is why you need to quickly evaluate your new employee during this narrow time frame. Staff feedback can be especially valuable at this stage. If given proper training, most employee performance does not radically change after the first month. Think back on individuals you have fired and if their performance changed from the first thirty days through the next year. Typically, your evaluation of what that employee contributes to the company will not likely be different over the next twelve months. If necessary, making a decision to fire that employee now will be less costly for the company and easier for the new employee over the long run.

Fire a customer. Companies need to fire customers that cost more than the revenue they are bringing in. Many times, these are the same ones that disrespect your employees, that you always talk negatively about, whose ethical behavior is not in line with your company values, and that prevent you from getting the customers that will sustain and grow your small business's reputation. When deciding which customers to fire, follow these warning signs:

1. **You are no longer really helping them.** Admit it. They are wasting

their money. These customers eventually will stop buying from you anyway, if there is no value in your services.

2. **The customer is disregarding your advice.** In this case, this can only end badly for your reputation, since eventually, they will blame you for their lack of success.

3. **The customer is not willing or able to pay a price that is profitable.** In addition, they may not be paying their bills on time or be willing to pay a profitable price. This is not the definition of the type of customer you need. In fact, this customer is preventing you from building a profitable company, and that affects all the other planned goals.

4. **The customer has asked you to do something illegal or unethical.** Regardless of what they promise to pay you, if the customer has behaved unethically or illegally, seek legal or HR advice and terminate their relationship.

5. **The customer has behaved inappropriately toward one of your employees.** This is another case where you need to get HR advice. Accepting this type of behavior is not a benefit to any business culture. And how employees act reflect on what you will tolerate.

That customer may be a large part of your revenue, so firing them needs to be done on your timetable by creating a termination plan. It should include identifying a series of potential prospects that can replace the problem customer. Begin to phase out the "fired" customer from your business when you start to gain these additional clients. Show the problem clients other "options for their needs" by even telling them they would be happier with your competitors. Set an internal date at which you will no longer be doing business with them. It is also important not to permit any personal discussion about these past customers by employees. This is just gossip and serves no business purpose. In a social media world, there is always a danger of this information getting back to past customers through current or former employees.

Revisit often. Regularly revisit the economic value of all employees, customers, and vendors. If you identify problems, waste no time in having a face-to-face discussion with them to set new business guidelines that can ensure their profitability. It is very difficult to change these situations, so they should be re-evaluated every three months.

CASE STUDY
ADD BY SUBTRACTING
FALCONDALE MOTORS*

Falcondale Motors has had many salespeople over the years. One salesperson, Erica, had been there a long time and had contributed greatly to the bottom line as part of a team effort. However, when the company started to expand and improve its infrastructure processes, Erica did not want to change the way she did business. She refused to use the new sales methods dictated by the team and would not record her activity in the company's new customer relationship management system. Overall, she was setting a bad example for the entire company, even though she was the leading sales producer.

The dealership owner brought an HR team in to help to document her goals and job descriptions. They set a 90-day improvement plan in motion. The manager and support staff became more involved in learning Erica's job, so when she did not meet the goals, she was fired and replaced by another sales rep. Fast-forward three months, and there is not a single employee or customer that misses Erica. In a year, no one will remember her.

*Fictional company

CHAPTER 18
You Hire for Skills, not Attitude

WHY YOU ARE STUCK

You don't know how to interview future employees. The entire process makes you uncomfortable since you were never trained to do this. In fact, you dislike the entire interviewing game. As a result, you only ask questions about their specific skills and past experiences. You never discuss their career goals and the goals of your business. You don't determine if they are actually a good fit into your company's culture. You have a tendency either to hire the candidate who wants the least amount of money, or who you liked the most.

You are in a rush to hire anyone to fill a job. You needed to fill that position yesterday, so you never created an annual hiring plan or a current job description. You only seek a new person when someone in the company quits or current employees are complaining so loudly about workload that it can no longer be ignored. You don't know where to look, so you post the job on Craigslist or pay a lot of money for a listing on another job board.

Your current culture does not match your ideal. You read a lot of business books, and you know what the culture in your company should be. Unfortunately, when doing an honest assessment, it is nowhere close to that and you don't know how to make the transition to what you need.

HOW TO GET UNSTUCK

Learn that skills can be taught, but attitude can't be bought. Herb Kelleher, former CEO of Southwest Airlines, said, *"We'll train you on* *whatever it is you have to do; but the one thing Southwest cannot change in people is inherent attitudes."* Always hire for overall fit into the organization. Skills can be taught to people who have an aptitude for learning in your environment. Attitude and fit into the corporate culture can't. First, determine how the candidate's attitude will meld into your organization's culture. This doesn't mean they will become duplicates of current employees, but instead how they will be complementary and help grow what the company currently has. Mark Murphy, author of *Hiring for Attitude*, tracked 20,000 new hires and found that 46% of them failed within eighteen months. He reports "89% of the time they failed for attitudinal reasons and only 11% of the time for a lack of skill."

Barbara Corcoran, who gained fame on the entrepreneurship show, *Shark Tank*, says, "The best people are honest and have lots of enthusiasm. Don't worry too much about their level of experience when you're interviewing, as the right attitude always delivers much more than just experience."

Early indications of people who have a hard time fitting in at a company include:

1. *Talking trash about their last company or boss.* If they are talking badly about them, then more than likely, if they become dissatisfied with your company, they will gossip about you.

2. *Frequent, annual job changes.* This is an indication that they were not able to adapt and add to the company culture. This also shows they do not know how to pick companies that they should be part of.

3. *Frequent use of "I" rather than "we."* An employee must be coachable If they always say, "I did this" rather than "we did this," they probably don't play well with others and are incapable of being coached by mentors.

Attitude feeds culture. It is such a critical part of building a successful culture. Mark Murphy says,

"Southwest, Google, Apple, and The Four Seasons are all great companies, and they all hire for attitude. Their high-performing employees live their attitudes every day and it's a big part of what makes these organizations so successful. Low performers [who] struggle with those attitudes are typically rejected by the culture. But those companies' attitudes are very different from each other. They couldn't successfully emulate each other's attitudes. Every company has to discover the attitudes that make their organization unique and special. And even if the company's attitudes change over the years, those attitudes will always be an organic reflection of their most successful people."

Count your characters. Do an honest, ongoing assessment of your culture and the employee personalities who make up your business. In any healthy company, you will find all these types of people:

- **Dreamers:** They come up with ideas and think of how customers can use the products and solutions.
- **Creators:** They create the products that customers envision.
- **Doers:** They get things done in the organization and don't ask a lot of questions. They are always ready to take tactical actions.
- **Talkers:** They may not get a lot done, but they know how to connect and rally other people to their cause.
- **Naysayers:** They are always saying "no" or playing devil's advocate in an argument.
- **Freeloaders:** They contribute nothing to the company and have either one foot out the door or shouldn't be there in the first place.

The successful company needs a combination of all these personalities. One person sometimes shares multiple roles. Think about where a particular candidate fits in and how they will interact with the rest of the group. Candidates with the right attitude have the following skills:

- **Courtesy:** Throughout hundreds of individual calls and interactions with customers and staff, can the employee remain courteous to each customer and to fellow team members? The customer who is on the phone (email or social media) doesn't care how many other customers the person has dealt with or if they are having a bad day. Can the employee set all this aside, start fresh with each interaction, and treat this customer with the courtesy they deserve?

- **Focus:** Does the employee have a proven ability to focus on a single task and follow it through to completion? Many customers complain that they constantly are passed around a company and have to explain an issue over and over again. When surveyed, this is always a very sore point for customers. This happens because a single problem may cross multiple departments. Can one employee be responsible for a task from beginning to end and not get distracted by other priorities?

- **Empathy:** Can employees put themselves in the customer's position, even if they think they are wrong? Can they truly say, "I understand how you see things your way." When calling a company, empathy is what customers truly want in order to be satisfied. Having the patience to listen to a customer rant will solve half their problem.

- **Calm:** Can the employee keep calm, even when the customer gets angry and begins to shout? Many people have a tendency to mirror the other person's reactions and ratchet up the emotion. This path never leads to effective customer service.

- **Improvise:** Can the employee improvise and not just be robotic by following a script and standard practices? Can they recognize when an exception to the rule needs to be made? Can they see the bigger profit picture and offer what is best for the customer and the company? Can they take responsibility for their decisions?

Write a clear job description. Don't just recycle old ones since roles and responsibilities constantly evolve in every small business. With each hire, take a fresh look at the business's needs and the skills that should be added to the team to accomplish the desired goal. Determine how this new hire will interact and help others on the same team.

Get referrals from satisfied employees. Paid job boards do have their role but not at the start because too many random resumes will be sent. You will spend too much time trying to identify viable candidates to interview. Instead, the best place to start is to ask internal resources. Remember that hiring truly is a team sport. Take advantage of the tools available inside the organization. Instruct employees to include a line in their email signature about the positions that are open and link it to your company website. Offer a monetary bounty after three months if the company hires based on a referral. Always have a "We are Hiring!" link on your home page. Use LinkedIn to become connected to viable candidates who are not currently looking for a job.

Shut up and listen in the interview. We all talk too much when meeting with new candidates because we are nervous. For many small business owners, they let their passion get the best of them and, as a result, they end up not shutting up about the company. Instead, make the interview very interactive, where the candidates do most of the talking. Give them an opportunity to ask questions. Team interviewing is always beneficial since one person's view may be different from another. It is also easier to listen while the other two people talk.

Always ask this one question: "Tell me about a time when . . ." Many people can give good interviews, but few can list specific, detailed success experiences. Here are some suggestions:

- **For sales reps:** "Tell me about a time when you were able to land a big new account." Or "tell me about a time when you lost an account."

- **For customer service reps:** "Tell me about a time when you were able to turn around a dissatisfied customer." Or "tell me about a time when a large customer left."

- **For a manager:** "Tell me about a time when you resolved a conflict with another employee." Or "tell me about a time when you fired an employee."

- **For a purchasing manager:** "Tell me about a time when you were able to build a long-term customer relationship." Or "tell me about a time when you had to reduce inventory or accounts receivables."

- **For a bookkeeper:** "Tell me about a time when the company did not have enough money to pay their bills."

Get examples that are as specific as possible by pressing for names, dates, and places.

Talk about money early. Do not leave this to the end or as the last step. Many people apply for jobs that are well below their salary range. Ensure that you do not waste your time by talking to candidates for whom the compensation would be too low or high. Be suspicious of people who will accept a job at 50% of their last compensation. Ask for a W-2 to verify their claimed pay.

Get referrals from references. Don't bother asking the candidate's references many questions. They will have been thoroughly prepped with how to answer. Ask that reference if they know anyone who can give the candidate a new reference. This referral will be more legitimate and less rehearsed.

Don't stop at references. Look candidates up in your favorite search engine. Find their profiles on LinkedIn, Facebook, Google Plus, and Twitter. What do their interactions with others in social media say about them? Also, get their permission to do a financial and criminal background check. While these results may not exclude them from employment, it is something that you should know with any incoming employee.

Formally train new employees. Early in my entrepreneurial career, the training for my new employees consisted of "Go build your own desk and then get started." This was not an optimal way to onboard employees. It is mandatory to have a real training program instead of just throwing a new hire into the deep end on the second day. This ensures their maximum contribution over the long-term. Train them on all the skills needed to be successful. This includes mastery of the processes and systems inside the company as well as its long-term values and goals.

This is the entire hiring and training process. If you are not comfortable that it can be done right, seek outside professional HR help.

CASE STUDY
CULTURE SERVED DAILY
NEXTIVA

Located just a few miles from Old Town Scottsdale, Arizona, is the sprawling office of Nextiva, a cloud-based phone service provider with more than 300 employees and very high retention rates. Five people started Nextiva in 2008 with a clear vision: to create a great place to work and deliver exemplary customer service. "Culture has been on our minds from the very beginning," says Yaniv Masjedi, a member of the founding team and Nextiva's vice president of marketing.

Open communication is the foundation of Nextiva's internal culture. Teams are kept small and employees are encouraged to share thoughts with their superiors at any time. The company releases an internal television episode dubbed "nexTV," every Friday that includes interviews with employees, jokes, and updates on sales efforts as well as acknowledgements of jobs well done.

The company's admirable office culture is a product of strict hiring criteria. Masjedi says they look for three things: "The person needs to be smart, a self-starter, and be passionate about working with great people and helping customers."

Once a candidate passes the test, they are welcomed with open arms into the Nextiva family and can look forward to not only the company's communicative culture but also free food, a game room (complete with a Ping-Pong table and pool table), and fun off-site events held regularly. Masjedi admits, "We all spend so much time at work that we wanted to make Nextiva a place where our employees liked coming every day."

CHAPTER 19

You Are Always Telling Employees What to Do Because You're the Boss

WHY YOU ARE STUCK

You think you have to instill fear to be successful. When thinking about what type of boss you wanted to be when you started your company, you point to well-worn successful examples like Donald "Your Fired" Trump and "Chainsaw" Al Dunlop, former CEO of Sunbeam and notorious downsizer. You admire the work of Steve Jobs who reportedly was a badgering and uncompromising micromanager whose blunt comments were known to sometimes reduce weaker employees to tears. Despite this harshness, Jobs extracted top performances from all sectors of Apple and forged it into one of the great companies of the millennium. Why can't you be like Jobs?

Throughout political history and in business, you think aggressive leaders have always run the show. These so-called "alphas" told their employees what to do and didn't much care about what they thought. They even threaten them with firing if the job didn't get done. You know it's not popular, but you believe that to get things done, a leader needs to be hard-nosed and sometimes cutthroat. You believe in the classic rule of evolution: only the strongest survive. You believe in a strict structure with narrowly defined steps up the corporate ladder. Compassion is really just about being soft, and you need to lead during tough times.

While many companies talk about rewards and encouragement, to really get things done, you think that most people are more motivated by punishment and criticism. You would never call yourself a bully, but success is your only option, and you will say and do anything to achieve it.[16] No employee can get in your way! You have heard of more collaborative styles, but they seem to take too much time. You would rather have loyalty from your employees, but you will settle for fear. The market is moving fast, and you have to be there. Besides, you don't think you can trust employees on their own without supervision.

You have created a culture of bullies. It comes as a bit of a surprise, but employees are now following your example. When you bully others and use an authoritative management style, others copy you. This makes you smile at first, but when you actually hear it coming from one of your managers, it does seem a bit harsh. You see this reflected online in company chats. And in meetings, there isn't much discussion when you are there. Other times, everyone seems to be angry at each other, or they focus on hard coercion tactics. In addition, you find your team quickly losing patience with customers and giving vendors ultimatums. This has created a high-pressure culture with increasing employee turnover and sick time.

HOW TO GET UNSTUCK

Don't try to be Steve Jobs. You are not and never will be Steve Jobs. While this is actually good news, many managers try to emulate famous leaders who really are one in a billion. Who knows what successful combination of personal and business factors came together for Jobs to make him legendary. Every small business owner has their own unique management style, competitors, and marketplace. You need to learn what works for you instead of imitating someone else's characteristics. In the long run, this is easier because employees are attracted to behavior that is more authentic.

Forget being an alpha. In an internet collaborative world, where there is increasing transparency, the alpha style is slowly dying. Dana Ardi, corporate anthropologist and author of *The Fall of the Alphas*, describes how beta managers are taking over the world. Alphas always take charge by aggressively making decisions and harshly communicating with others. Betas don't communicate as harshly, but instead stress cooperation with their peers and employees. Alphas intimidate to accomplish their goals, while betas engage to find a winning scenario most people can support. Alphas promote relentless competition among employees, while betas encourage teamwork. Successful leaders now build internal and external communities rather than a cutthroat, winner-takes-all work environment.

For example, one of Zappos' core values is to build relationships with customers, vendors, and fellow employees through open and honest communication. That's not just a nice thing to do; it's company policy. Manish Patel, CEO of digital marketer Where 2 Get It, is so committed to his employees performing community service, he pays them for it.

This new way of leading and building a company already seems to be affecting not only companies but how these skills are taught at business schools. Take a look at some classes at the University of Chicago, and you will find that a key skill to be developed is learning how to work as a group. Each student concentrates on their strengths to contribute to the groups' overall success. The students in Chicago even fly to London and Singapore to meet and connect with other University of Chicago business students abroad. When I was at Northwestern business school, I thought collaboration was the best skill I learned.

In a globally connected world, cooperation between allies and competitors has become more profitable. This is why the beta-type leaders will someday rule the business world. Accept this trend in your own company if you want to maximize performance and results. While a company should never pretend to be a democracy, always lead by building consensus when possible. Ask others' their solution before making a final decision. Know how to delegate your weaker areas and then stay out of way. Alphas can sometimes manage by fear, but employees don't stay in these situations long if they have other options. Regardless of the economic climate, the best people can always find new opportunities. Alphas can never gain what really matters in building the best team: loyalty. History shows that loyalty to a person, group, or cause is the strongest bond and produces the most dedicated, long-term action.

Watch it, though: Betas can be a bust, too. Ardi writes that beta companies have disadvantages if poorly implemented. She says, "Many leaders feel loss of control. Many employees, if not properly considered and self-motivated, feel role confusion. Coordination and organizational learning must occur or there will be confusion." If this is only a Zen-touchy-feely-holistic management style, where everyone sits in a circle and holds hands, it will definitely fail. Any shift from one management style to the other needs to be done gradually.

Now, throw out the bullies. Does that include you? If the answer is "maybe," it's time to evaluate your personal behavior, management style, and its overall effect on the organization. It starts by changing your behavior, how you have discussions, and then how decisions are ultimately made. Realize what bullying costs the company in work productivity, culture, and company loyalty. Who truly works to their potential over a long period of time in an environment that fosters fear? Small business expert, Seth Godin says,

"An organization that is built on ideas and connection can't thrive when there's a bully in the room. [They] drive away some of your best employees, because they can most easily find another place to work. He also silences the eager and the earnest, the people with great ideas who are now too intimidated to bother sharing them. His behavior has robbed your organization of the insight that could open so many doors in the future. The bully works to marginalize

people. In an organizational setting, the bully chooses not to engage in conversation or discussion, or to use legitimate authority or persuasion, and depends instead on pressure in the moment to demean and disrespect someone else—by undermining not just their ideas, but their very presence and legitimacy."

Fire the bullies and recognize their true cost to your company in employee turnover, lost customers, and unhappy vendors.

Learn how women do it. According to many studies, women more effectively manage companies through their beta style. Here are some of the reasons why:

- **They are better communicators.** Women are better listeners than men, and this is exactly the skill that is most critical for managing employees and customers. Attend any dinner party where the men and women are talking in separate rooms. The women are listening to each other, and the men are competing with each other by talking about their jobs, cars, or power tools. According to Dr. Susan Sherwood, this is a result of women being more discussion-oriented and men wanting to just take action. Men communicate through activities rather than conversations. Unfortunately, employees want their manager first to hear their point of view before they act. Customers want companies to empathize with their problem before they find a solution. Being a better communicator will lead to a stronger relationship of trust, which is critical to establishing loyalty.

- **They are focused on community.** Women are better consensus builders and don't have the need, like men, to direct everyone in what to do. Unlike men, they are just as comfortable giving away the credit as taking it. Ardi says the best managers learn to lead through the influence that comes from building a larger community rather than straight force or all-out intense competition.

- **They are more ethical.** Women as effective managers are better at considering the fair rights of others. Running a small business is always a minefield of ethical choices. When pushed to the limit, many owners do the wrong thing and run askew of their own ethical (and sometimes legal) standards. A strong base of business ethics will help the business owner deal with these types of challenges, which will certainly push them to their limit. I remember when I started my first company; my partner and I took our wives out to dinner. We talked about the dream of building a business; how we would be different from our previous bosses. There were certain ethical lines that we would never cross. We discussed different scenarios and situations. I distinctly remember our answers from that evening. We detailed what we would do and what we would not do. In the next five years, we stepped over that gray line and back repeatedly. Our responses to the situations as they arose bore little resemblance to what we had said that evening.

- **They have patience.** Women are far more patient with employees than men. They are less likely to jump to an immediate conclusion and make a quick decision or take action too soon. A study commissioned by parcel and courier service myHermes, showed that women are willing to wait longer for a desired result. The winners are consistently the ones that can be patient enough to take actions, which result in small steps toward a specific goal.

- **They are better at activating passion.** According to Jay Forte, author of *Fire Up! Your Employees and Smoke Your Competition*, women are "more astute about knowing how to activate passion in their employees. They watch the forty-three muscles in your face and see how your emotions change." In both customers and employees, passion for a product or service builds loyalty and sustainability.

As Sarah Robinson describes in her book *Fierce Loyalty,* in a social media world where most consumers check reputation online before buying, a passionate community among employees and customers is the strongest marketing strategy for any business.

CASE STUDY
COLLABORATING VIRTUALLY
ARMENT DIETRICH

In November 2011, Gini Dietrich took her integrated marketing communications business completely virtual. The reason was to save money and build her cash reserves after the economy began to rebound. The idea was to test it out for a year and then go back to standard brick-and-mortar office space. But when the team considered going back to a physical office space, they decided to stay virtual.

However, collaborating virtually has its challenges. It was difficult for Dietrich to change her thinking from being able to see people at their desks working to not caring about when or where they work, as long as they are productive and accomplish their goals. It also prevented the beneficial, impromptu conversations that happen while making coffee or filling a water bottle.

To manage those challenges and continue to build a collaborative environment, Dietrich does the following:

- They use Apple iMessaging across all devices. Her team is all on a favorites list that provides them the opportunity to gain one another's attention very quickly.

- They do direct report meetings via Skype, which provides the feeling that both team members are in the same room.

- Staff meetings are done via Google Hangouts so they can all see one another, read body language, and get things accomplished.

- Every Thursday afternoon, they have "wine: thirty," which is an informal, no-agenda staff meeting.

- Some of her team even keep Skype video open all day so it feels like their colleagues are sitting at the next desk.

Because of technology and their commitment to making it work, Dietrich's team is actually more collaborative in this environment than they ever were all in the same office.

CHAPTER 20

You Think Customer Service Is a Cost Center

WHY YOU ARE STUCK

While watching the front door, you leave the back one open. You are so focused on bringing new customers in the front door, that you leave the back door wide open for them to leave. You spend all your resources on attracting new customers and don't think about how to keep the ones you have. In fact, you focus all your sales and marketing on finding and selling new prospects. You forget about the lifetime value of a customer, and how expensive it is to get new customers versus keeping the ones you have.

You think customer service is a necessary evil. You place no value on servicing existing customers. You think people who call and email are only there to complain or get something free. Therefore, you provide the minimum service, so it does not subtract from the company's profits.

You want to match Amazon's customer service model. But you don't have the resources to do it like Amazon and Zappos. Unfortunately, this is what you think all consumers expect, so when you can't make this type of investment, you simply stop focusing on customer service.

HOW TO GET UNSTUCK

Customer service is the new marketing. As discussed in Chapter 12, reputation is one of the most important tools in marketing. Customer service is a key component in building an incredible company reputation that keeps people loyal. What gets and keeps people buying a product has changed. For most of the last century, consumers believed what a company said in its advertisements. A business might hire an advertising agency on Madison Avenue (like "Mad Men") to come up with a catchy slogan delivered by a celebrity in order to influence what the customer would buy.

Today, the Internet has allowed society to move from this one-way medium to a more interactive buying process. According to BIA/ Kelsey Group, an astounding 97% of customers review products online before buying. But what may be even more of a surprise is the information they are researching. Consumers are not only looking at the latest features, prices, and availability, but they also want to know what other consumers are saying about the product and the company. Today, these reviews have a higher level of credibility than any company-directed advertising, and most directly influence what the consumer eventually buys. As previously discussed, 92% of consumers say they trust "earned media" (word of mouth and recommendations from friends), which is far ahead of all other forms of advertising.

This peer-review system has become familiar with anyone using sites, such as Amazon, eBay, TripAdvisor, Yahoo! Local, or Yelp. Consumers value the "human voice" more than any corporate messaging. In addition, Google and Yahoo! search engine results about a particular company or product never fade; they can be found forever.

As discussed in Chapter 13, the immediate electronic delivery of products and fast worldwide shipments of goods makes most products commodities, since they are available across vast geographies. Price competition has become intense. This presents a huge challenge for most small business owners because their competitors can now be anywhere in the world. As a result, the only truly sustainable competitive advantage for any small business is their customer service. In fact, according to American Express survey, 70% of customers are willing to spend more with companies that provide excellent customer service.

Improve each customer communication. B.C. (before computers) business owners sent letters, called on the phone, or visited a customer in person. There really were only these three ways to "talk." As a result, business communication was much simpler. Now customers can contact a business through chat, social media, email, voice mail, and fax. With a smartphone in every customer's hand, there are so many ways to communicate at any time of the day or night. What makes it even more difficult is that customers expect an answer immediately, and most small businesses stink at communicating with customers. They don't have a unified plan to monitor all communication channels, and they don't get back to customers in a timely fashion by the same team of people. You cannot afford to make these mistakes. Customer response time has a big impact on a small business's reputation and, therefore, sales.

Your company does not have to be Amazon, but you can still improve communication:

- **Email should be replied to now.** Do you know which email address customers use the most when they expect to receive a reply from a customer service rep? If you do not, figure it out or assign one. Then put an immediate auto responder on it, saying how long it will take for someone to get back to the customer—and make darn sure a rep replies within the specified time!

- **Only offer chat if it can be staffed for an extended period of time.** Review website traffic and find out when a majority of users visit. Be careful when outsourcing this function since the company may not have enough information to really help the customer. Do not offer mobile phone chat unless this is the targeted customers' favorite form of communication. (Typically, that's reserved for consumers under twenty-five years old.)

- **When the customer calls, have a live person nearby.** Depending on the volume of calls, it may not be practical to have every caller be answered live. However, automated answer trees should be limited and only have one level before accessing a live person. There is nothing more frustrating than "voice mail jail," where a real person is always just out of reach.

- **Make all calls "first and final."** Whoever "catches" the first communication message from the customer should track it through to completion. The biggest complaint most people have when they call a company is they are passed off to someone else and have to explain their issue all over again.

Consumers are talking online about your business—make sure it's positive.

The familiar statistic was that an unhappy customer would tell seven people. Now through social media and online review sites, they can tell millions! Remember when United Airlines broke Dave Carroll's guitar? He produced a video that was seen by seven million people and negatively impacted that corporation's stock price.

Boost your customer service—and get great online reviews—by following these four steps:

1. **Listen and learn.** Sign up for Google Alerts or for a trusted reputation management service, like those available from Dex One and SuperMedia, to see what people are saying about your business (and your competitors). Let go of the fear of what your customers' are saying and track your reputation across the entire web. Read the good *and* bad comments, so you can be ready to take action.

2. **Engage constructively.** Thank your business's fans and encourage them to spread the word about your company. Answer comments

from your business critics by acknowledging the issue and offering a remedy, if appropriate. Remaining silent to critics is not an advantage. When flying, I always get excellent help on the Twitter feed from American Airlines, which employs dozens of people around the clock to monitor it. They are using this customer service tool to try to turn around the perception of an industry that typically does not communicate well.

3. **Join the conversation.** Be helpful in any area where your business has expertise. Give advice frequently without selling anything. This will solidify your relationships with customers and prospects so they are more likely to buy from you when they need your service.

4. **Track it over time.** See if your social media efforts are leading to comments that are more positive. Find out where the comments and reviews are coming from so you can focus your attention (and possibly your advertising) on those sites.

Turn customer service into a profit center. Think about how much money your company makes over the lifetime of a customer. Smart companies invest in this area because it makes them money in the long run. The value of the customer to the company is not just from the initial sale but all the follow-on ones as well. Customer service is what keeps them coming back for more and referring others. A customer's overall economic value can be from the following:

- Revenue or the time of year that revenue is realized. An order in December when the company is at full capacity may not be as valuable as one in the slower summer months.

- Referrals or positive word of mouth. Having that customer as a brand and reference can build your company.

- Honest feedback provided to your company to help improve your products or services. This can translate into profits (or save lots of money) in the future.

Enter the new Golden Age of Customer Service.

Take advantage of new technology tools to offer unparalleled personalization and information access to customers. Armed with these new tools, small businesses can now project a full-service commitment in the age of self-service. Here are some of the services you will be able to offer.

- **Greet customers by name:** In the past, small business owners knew all their customers by name when they walked into their store or office. Now with web browser cookie technology, every company can call their customers by name on their website if they visited before. As a result, companies can even suggest what customers should buy in the future. This "faux personalization" is preferred by customers more than repeatedly visiting a local retail franchise where the sales rep has no idea who they are.

- **Answer questions 24/7:** In the past, customers would call or write a company, then wait weeks for a reply. Today, companies can assist customers with helping themselves through online FAQs, video demos, and chat. Well-designed self-service information on the Internet can aid customers any time day or night and provide an answer immediately.

- **Offer personalization:** A hundred years ago, a consumer could get a Ford Model T "in any color as long as it was black" according to Henry Ford. Now, most products are customized through technology so a customer can personalize it when they need it. For example, consumers can design their own Nike shoes, mix their own flavors at a Coca-Cola Freestyle machine, or customize a single copy of a book on Amazon.

- **Ship products same day:** In the old days, to get a product, the customer had to travel to pick it up at the retail location or wait weeks or months for delivery. Today, a customer cannot only get it sent the same day,[17] but also frequently get it shipped free of charge! Major companies like Amazon and Walmart also offer same-day delivery. In the printing world, new 3D-printing technology is allowing consumers to "print out" many products themselves.

- **Bring clothes buying to the home or office:** Customers no longer have to travel to a store to try on clothes to get the best fit. Today, there is an app for that! It's a simple as getting the mobile app, then uploading a photo and body specs. The consumer can then choose clothing to see how it fits without leaving their home or office. Need help? Personal online shopping assistants are available to help with the purchase decision.

CASE STUDY
EVERYDAY AMAZING SERVICE
NEXTIVA

While phone service companies haven't historically been known for their stellar customer service, that paradigm shifted at Nextiva, a cloud-based provider in Scottsdale, Arizona. Among the founding team's most prominent priorities was to offer a level of service that surpassed competitors, dubbing the concept "Amazing Service." But instead of designing the customer service department as a cost center (that is, an avenue to upsell vulnerable customers), Nextiva went in another direction entirely.

"We utilize our customer service department as a marketing tool," says Yaniv Masjedi, Nextiva's vice president of marketing. The company's social media presence is a perfect example. A quick glance at its Facebook page reveals hundreds of thank you posts from customers, followed by responses from Nextiva employees, with links to 15-second videos of employees thanking individual customers. "Those videos have been awesome for us," says Masjedi. "They really showcase our dedication to our customers."

Happy customers tend to spread the word, he says, which brings even more people to the Nextiva website and social media pages. The company also has a policy of reaching out to such customers with referral incentives, thereby extending the reach of a satisfied client base and continuing the positive cycle built entirely on the company's culture of "Amazing Service." Masjedi believes that "our referral program and social media interactions are a testament to how well our customer service team is doing. It is our first priority."

CHAPTER 21
You Never Ask for Help

WHY YOU ARE STUCK

You think you know everything. Mark Twain said, "It ain't what you don't know that gets you into trouble. It's what you know for sure that just ain't so." As the founder, you feel that you need to know everything. As the senior member of the team, you think that true leaders have almost omnipotent knowledge of their business.

You know it's lonely at the top. You accepted this responsibility when you got started. As a small business owner, you think the buck stops with you and you must make all the important decisions alone. There are many nights you wake up in a cold sweat thinking about the enormity of the responsibilities you face. In your mind, it is acceptable to listen to others' ideas, but the pressure is always on you at the top. At the end of the day, you are the one sitting alone in your office making a decision long past when everyone else has gone home.

You believe that asking for help is a sign of weakness. You think that small business ownership is a solo sport. You feel solely responsible for everything that happens at the company, and you do not believe you should burden anyone else. Asking for help will expose to others that you really don't have it all mapped out. You don't want people to find out that you are just making it up as you go along. Due to your shyness, asking for any kind of help has always been an issue since you were young. Being an introvert, you were always forced to figure things out on your own. This has become easier by surfing the Internet. You have survived by finding articles and videos to learn many of the things you need to know to run the company. Somehow, though, you miss bouncing ideas off another person who won't judge you.

You will feel stupid. In your mind, leaders are smarter than everyone else. You feel that if you ask people for help, they will realize that you really don't know everything. This will hurt their confidence in you and affect your ability to lead the team. You suffer from what is commonly called the impostor syndrome. You don't want to be found out as the fraud you really feel like sometimes. The last thing you want is to be judged by anyone and have your authority questioned because of your lack of knowledge.

You don't know anyone who can help. You don't even know where to start looking and who you can trust. Your accountant and lawyer are expensive and don't really understand the business from an owner's perspective. You can't go to your banker because if she knew what was really going on inside your company and your head, she never would lend the business money again. You don't want to ask friends because you are careful not to mix business and pleasure. You feel more comfortable not asking for favors so you don't owe anyone anything. You made it this far "on your own," and you don't want to be dependent on others.

HOW TO GET UNSTUCK

Find a trusted mentor. Many small business owners repeat that the one key element to their success is finding and working with the right mentor. Many leaders find it difficult to get the unfiltered advice they need while making critical decisions for their company. A manager or employee may give an important perspective, but they are always hampered by the fact that they work for you. A mentor is the person (or group of people) who becomes the trusted outside voice a business owner can rely on through good times and bad. It is not someone you will fire when things go south, but rather an annual commitment to stay with them.

Start by reaching out. Asking for help is what smart small business owners do, and you will be surprised how many people will say yes. Remember, you are under no obligation to take all their help, but rather take the pieces that fit best. Start by thinking about the people you respect that may have expertise in the area you need. Email or call them to say, "I am having a hard time with (salespeople, cash flow, inventory management), can you spend fifteen minutes on the phone with me?" Ask for a very small commitment of their time initially, and don't make it too formal. The best way to benefit from this conversation is to write down specific questions to ask the mentor in advance. Be as detailed as possible, and prepare follow-up questions based on their answers. The mentor will probably ask a series of questions you can't answer on the spot. Write those down, and do the research before asking the person for help again. Complete the circle by always letting the advisor know the results of their advice.

If you look, mentors are all around you. They could be a peer who has run their own business and felt your pain. Nothing can be substituted for having the opportunity to vent or talk things through with someone who is not involved in your business every day or who does not have it "all on the line" like you do. It will help vaporize your isolation and give you support when it is needed most. Mentors can be your unofficial therapist or your unwed partner in your business adventure. They can be a member of your local chamber of commerce, a peer at a networking group, or an advisor at your local SCORE chapter or Small Business Development Center (SBDC).

What qualities should a mentor have? Primarily, they must be able to patiently listen to you. After fifteen years of personal and group therapy, I realized that what I was mostly paying for was the rights to have someone listen to me without judgment. It was expensive—and worth it! The process of articulating your thoughts from your head to your mouth for others to hear as a sounding board can help a lot. Many times, you don't need additional ideas, just the opportunity to articulate it in front of someone. Your mentor should be someone who communicates in a way that will not make you feel stupid, no matter what you say. The environment surrounding any conversation with a mentor should also feel safe. You should be able to say anything in confidence and know that it goes no further than the two of you. Finally, there must be mutual respect. Forget about older and wiser. Do you respect their point of view? Are they truly interested in your definition of personal and business success? You may not agree with their point of view. But can you trust they are trying to be helpful?

Admit what you don't know. This is probably one of the most difficult admissions for a successful business owner to understand. What are your best skills, and where do you need help? It is always more challenging to find out what you truly don't know than what you are certain you do know. Many times, it's hard to figure this out from inside a company. Ask past employees and managers for an evaluation (current ones will be too afraid to be honest unless it's anonymous). Owners can even take skill evaluation tests like Meyers-Briggs to help in this area.

Get a collaborator. Leaders learn in different ways. Some like to read about how to perform new skills. Others want that skill demonstrated or to visually see a diagram of the process. A business owner needs to find a mentor who can teach the way they most easily learn. This becomes the core of effective collaboration. Does the way they teach get you unstuck and move your perspective of the problem to another place? In the beginning, meeting biweekly is important so they can learn how you work. Thereafter, meeting at least monthly is important for continuity.

Can you give your trust? Gaining and giving business trust is an inexact science. You need to understand at what point you freely give your trust. Is it a result of experience with that person or just personal interactions? Do their education qualifications matter or just their business experience? Some people easily give trust when someone they know refers that person. Ultimately, if you don't trust the mentor, then any advice they give will be ignored or marginalized. It is easier to give a bit of trust at a time. Start with a small problem, and use their advice to take action. If that process works well, bring bigger issues.

How do I compensate mentors? Some believe they will get the most unbiased advice if they do not pay their mentors. They think that anyone paid to help them will only offer information they want to hear. I believe the best option is to pay a mentor because they will be more focused and responsive. This can be accomplished with cash or a business trade. For the business owner, people value and respect what they have to pay for. Using a paid mentor, you will prepare and respect this activity much more. In turn, your commitment will yield better long-term results.

Truly listen—don't give lip service. One of the hallmarks of a great small business leader is the ability to listen to others. This doesn't just mean giving the mentor their "say" but really discovering how their opinion fits and influences your important decisions. Many small business owners have developed a talent of appearing to listen, but their mind is already made up or they are truly thinking about something else. Can you stop the justification for a pending decision in your head and accept an alternate point of view? The right mentor may take months or years to find. There is never a need to be in a rush for the best fit.

CASE STUDY

A SECOND OPINION

RICK MAZURSKY

Rick Mazursky was always one of my favorite mentors. I could always count on him as my "business ethics" meter and guide me to do the right thing when I got off-course. I chose Mazursky because he has built long-term relationships. With forty-five years of experience in product design and development, marketing, domestic and international distribution, he has seen almost everything. Mazursky has held leadership positions in companies involved in the creation and distribution of products to consumers and has served as president of VTech Industries. He grew the business from a struggling midsize company to one of the top toy companies in the world. Whenever Mazursky starts working at a new place, he brings trusted members of other teams to be with him. For example, he has used the same vice president of sales at three different companies. And for the past twenty-five years, Mazursky has used the same product development manager, graphic artists, packaging specialists, and model makers across many projects. In turn, all these people have used the same teams: the same sales force, ad agency, product developers, and factories. It has become a trusted workforce.

What I liked about working with Mazursky is that he never judged me. He's offered multiple points of view but never made a decision for me. Mazursky had always been there when I needed him but never pushed his way into my companies or insisted on a particular solution. In short, he was the perfect mentor.

CHAPTER 22

You Allow Personal Use of Smartphones on the Job

WHY YOU ARE STUCK

You let it. You do not have any rules in place for smartphones that are being used during work hours. You see people using them on the job, but you have a difficult time figuring out what they are doing on them that is business related. Your company has never had a policy for them since you don't want to seem like Big Brother. When you see it happening, you don't say anything, yet you sense that using smartphones keeps employees distracted from effectively doing their best work. You think your customers are annoyed when they enter your retail or office space and the customer-facing staff always seem to be tapping something into their smartphones. Customers seem afraid to ask questions for fear of interrupting them. This is all bad news. But what can you do?

You get frustrated and take no action. But you feel powerless to do anything about it. You feel bad about intruding into their personal lives and know how attached most people are to their phones. However, you can't help feeling this activity does not allow them to focus on their job. You are stuck because you worry about the employee backlash if you don't let them use their phones. You want to give your employees the room to get their job done any way they can as long as the results are there, but smartphone usage is not creating an environment that is conducive to this.

HOW TO GET UNSTUCK

Control the attraction to distraction at your business. Mobile technology has become a defining feature of modern living at home and the office like PDAs or pagers did ten years ago. Smartphones give everyone the same power to communicate—only multiply that by 100 because of near-universal Internet access and thousands of additional applications. Although the Internet made communicating and sharing information much easier, it also added dozens of potential distractions. Despite all the promised potential that smartphones have to make your business run more efficiently, they contain just as much potential to disrupt productivity and make your business an unorganized mess. Years ago, having games and Internet access available on an office computer was bad enough, but now having all this and more available on a pocket-sized device is a business nightmare. There is no way smartphone usage can be monitored easily or ethically. To save your employees from temptation, it's important for you to step up and create ground rules for smartphone usage inside your company.

Separate and focus. The first question that needs to be evaluated is—does the employee really need their smartphone for business reasons? Not for emergencies, but in the course of their everyday responsibilities. If the answer is no, then there is no reason they should have it during work hours. This activity would be similar to talking on the phone to a friend when they are supposed to be working. Unfortunately, the distraction of the smartphone permeates through almost every profession. I have witnessed all these things personally:

- Hotel or high-rise doorman and security guards sometimes watch their phones instead of the people around them.

- TSA personnel at times check their phones instead of screening passengers. I personally reported a TSA officer who was looking at the screening computer *and* checking their cell phone.

- Cleaning crews who are talking on their phones while doing their jobs or pushing their carts from one place to the next.

- Taxi drivers who are always on their phones and, therefore, can't hear where a passenger wants to be driven.

- Flight attendants are sometimes on their smartphones while passengers are boarding the airplane instead of helping.

- Airline baggage personnel have their phone tucked underneath their noise-canceling headphones sometimes so they can talk while loading the airplane.

Constant monitoring of a smartphone is not good for an individual's concentration and does not allow them an environment to do their best job. While there are so many advantages to having a smartphone, overall, doing their job better is typically just not one of them. In 2005, Hewlett-Packard and the Institute of Psychiatry at the University of London completed a study where employees who were distracted by incoming email and phone calls saw a 10-point fall in their IQ. This is more than the impact of smoking marijuana! A 2013 study by Michigan State University confirms that interruptions of 2.8 seconds double the likelihood that an employee will make an error. If the distraction is lengthened to 4.4 seconds, the number of mistakes triples. Microsoft found that it took fifteen minutes for employees to return to serious work tasks after responding to an incoming email or text.

Issue a separate phone for business. It is a very common practice now for employees to bring their own device (BYOD) to work. This complicates smartphone usage if the employee is required to use the same device for business and personal use. If there is a company need, don't have employees use their own smartphone for work. Buy them a separate device and limit the applications on that phone to business-only use. Periodically track what it is being used for, including email, text, phone, and social media activities. While this may be a bit more expensive for employers and inconvenient for employees, the cost will be more than made up in increased focus and productivity.

Leave the phone out of meetings. Constant smartphone usage at a company can become negatively ingrained in the culture. At these businesses, employees will be distracted by smartphones during group or one-on-one meetings. Again, the message that constant use of a smartphone sends is that whatever the next interruption is takes precedent over what is being done right now. Advise all employees to leave their phones at their desk or turn them off when coming to any type of meeting.

Keep it in their pocket. Set clear rules that smartphones are not to be taken out unless there is an emergency. Clearly state all smartphones are subject to the employer's social media, internet, and other computer-related policies. Employees can't use them for personal calls during work or to check their social media status. Make it clear that there is simply no privacy at work. But phones can be used on work breaks or in designated areas. While the U.S. First Amendment protects freedom of speech from being limited by the government; it does not apply to the case of small businesses. Have specific consequences for using personal smartphones at work, which include terminating employment.

Ban them. This is becoming a more common policy at American businesses. It should be an easy decision for employees involved in driving or using machinery at a company. It is also becoming a problem among employees in open office settings. A recent survey by staffing company Ranstad USA and the Society for Human Resource Management, reported 30% of employees cited cell phones ringing at work as their number-one pet peeve. Remember, phones don't just ring anymore, but can use a wide variety of distracting ringtones.

Some FedEx locations are prohibiting personal cell phones at work. Employees at its Indianapolis transportation hub were told not to bring their phones into the building. According to "Work Life Web 2011," a report by information security company Clearswift, 33% of Australian workplaces block or discourage the use of social media while in the office. This is up over 50% from the previous year.

Another reason companies are banning cell phones is because they also have cameras, and they don't want their intellectual property stolen. Employee smartphones pose an additional risk that information will be copied and eventually sent to competitors or posted on the Internet. This is especially important to companies that have trade secrets. Sexual harassment can also increase with texting, since many times people will type what they won't say in person.

If an employee sits at a desk all day, there is no reason to pull out their smartphone. For example, an employee can search for something on Google or chat with other employees, right on their computer desktop. While an outright ban may seem draconian at first, it's not without precedent as described above. Many other employers have banned smartphones, and while employees get angry at first, it passes quickly. Make this policy clear in the hiring process. The ban should include personal conversations, playing games, surfing the Internet, checking social media feeds, and sending and receiving text messages. While many employees are very attached to their phones, most of them understand that when they're in the office, their time belongs to the company. As long as your policy is fair and enforced on everyone, it should not be an issue after a few months.[18] This policy should also apply to contractors and other temporary workers who work at your site, as well as you and the entire management team. Ultimately, a complete ban is easier because there is no realistic way for any employer to monitor personal smartphone usage on a consistent basis without feeling like a school hall monitor.

According to safety consultant Brian Irlam, this issue has actually been brought to court when employees have been deprived of their phone.

Since many people rely on their cell phones to communicate with friends and family while at work, an argument could be made that restricting cell phone use is discrimination against workers with families. In fact, one worker brought such a case against their employer and lost. It was filed by a construction company worker. They claimed the company's policy of banning workers from carrying phones was family-status discrimination because it prevented his mother, who didn't speak English, from contacting him. The company and employee eventually reached a compromise where the worker was allowed to take his cell phone onto the site, if he set it to vibrate, and agreed only to use it in designated areas.

Implement the policy, and watch productivity soar. Tell employees why the policy is being implemented. Show examples of other companies and get their feedback. Write out the policy, and make it part of the company's HR manual. Remember a separate policy may be needed for employees who drive cars or machinery as part of their work responsibilities. Have employees acknowledge they received the updated manual by signing a form. Enforce it consistently with predetermined consequences. After three months, survey employees to gather information on their increased productivity as a result of the ban. You will be surprised at the results.

Send a strong signal to customers. Think about the message an employee using a smartphone sends a customer. Instead of being welcoming and helpful, it means "I am busy here; don't bother me." This is never a way that a person interested in doing business with your company should be treated. When an employee isn't using their smartphone, they also can focus on attracting customers in person, on the web, by phone, or email.

CASE STUDY

OUT IN FRONT

MENARDS

I walk into many stores where the sales clerk is either on a personal call or trying to hide their smartphone usage below a countertop. I always feel like I am interrupting or I feel sorry for the owner who is paying for an employee who is here in body, but not in effort.

At Menards, a national home improvement retailer, sales clerks and cashiers are never allowed to use cell phones on the selling floor. In fact, when a cashier has no one in their line, they don't immediately whip out their cell phone as so many waiting retail clerks do. Instead, they move from behind their cash register to the front of their station to show approaching customers they are available to help. Which scenario is more appealing to you as a potential customer?

CHAPTER 23

You Don't Know How to Read
Your Financial Statements

WHY YOU ARE STUCK

You never review your financials. You never learned to read them, and you seem to be getting along just fine without them. Once a year, you bring in your accountant and she tells you what you need to know. You don't ask her for help because either she doesn't explain them well or she makes you feel stupid when you ask a question. You are not even sure how these statements relate to running a business. You ultimately brush it off since you think you have a good idea of what the "real numbers" are in your head. As a result, you make all business decisions blindly.

Your financial decisions are ruled by emotions. You do what feels right. This means either feeding your own ego or taking care of the company's squeaky wheel. This leads to borrowing and spending money based on expected results, which only gets you into overwhelming debt.

You think business success is about revenue, not cash flow. You only focus on the top sales number. As long as this is growing, you think your business will be successful. You believe that ultimately some of this money must trickle down to your own pocket.

You don't share financial information with your employees. You don't share much financial information with your employees because it is paradoxical. Will disclosing information that shows the company earning a lot of money make employees jealous? Will they then ask for raises? Alternately, if the company is having financial problems, will employees get worried and start to look for other jobs?

HOW TO GET UNSTUCK

Learn to read a profit and loss statement (also called the income statement).

Get over your fear of the numbers. A financial statement shows the revenue, expenses, and profit of a business over a period of time. Following are the basic components:

- *Revenue:* This is a business's sales, which result from any customer that buys products or services.

- *Cost of goods or services (COGS):* This is defined as the direct cost of producing the product or service the business sells and could be raw materials or labor.

- *Gross profit:* The difference between sales and cost of goods is also known as the gross margin.

- *General expenses:* Rent, people, insurance, utilities, telephone, travel, etc.

- *Net profit:* This is the difference between gross profit and general expenses. Taxes and depreciation are typically deducted from net profit.

Learn to read a balance sheet.

This is the book value of your business at any given point in time. It also measures the ability of a company to pay its debts. Following are the basic components:

Assets: What the company owns. This can include:

- *Cash:* How much money the company has in the bank

- *Accounts receivable:* The value and age of the money that is owed the business

- *Inventory:* The value of the inventory
- *Fixed assets:* Equipment, computers, and property

Liabilities: What the company owes. This can include:

- *Accounts payable:* The money the business owes vendors
- *Loans:* The money the company owes banks and other sources

Owners' Equity: The assets minus the liabilities. This can include:

- *Stock:* Paid-in capital
- *Retained earnings:* Profit retained in the company since the start

There are many good resources available to learn to read financial statements.[19] Get help from your CPA or educate yourself online. Remember, accountants are advisors, not adversaries.

Review your financial statements on a monthly basis. Performing this task every month will help you gauge the health of your business. Here are three other measurements to find out important information about your business:

1. *The quick ratio (or the acid test) on the balance sheet*: This is the business's current amount of assets (cash, cash equivalents, accounts receivables) divided by current liabilities. A favored metric of banks, the quick ratio is a measure of the financial stability of a business. In most industries, the quick ratio should be greater than 1. It shows that the company has more cash available than current money it owes. When the ratio goes below 1, it means your business may not be able to meet its financial commitments.

2. *The business' sales-close ratio in your customer relationship management system (CRM)*: Of all the proposals your business sends, how

many do you win? This is a key number since it should not be too low or too high. If it is too high, either your business is not talking to enough prospects or your prices are too low. If it is too low, you may not be qualifying your prospects enough before preparing proposals for them.

3. *Your ten most important customers:* While this may start on the profit and loss statement, this is measured not only by revenue but also by their referrals, the additional products they buy, feedback they give, retention, or their superior brand power.

Don't let too much money makes you stupid. More small business owners get stupid when they become financially successful. They start to throw money at a problem instead of using their creative brainpower to solve it. Be cheap; it's your money. Do a small test first and get those results. If it is successful, invest more money to expand its effect or take the next step.

Build first, get rich later. Too many small business owners worry about getting rich quick and selling their business. Overnight success takes years to achieve. Build value in your company and eventually someone will pay for it.

Set budgets twice. Budgets are an important part of financial management, but many small business owners use this tool wrong. They set an annual budget, but then adjust it every month if their results do not match. Stop doing this! Set a budget before the beginning of a fiscal year. Compare results, and only reset the budget at midyear. Budgets are useless if they are reset to match results every month.

Share financial information with your employees. Most new business owners limit disclosing any financial information. But over time, they begin to understand that a certain level of this type of information needs to be shared with their employees to get commitment to the company's mission. Any information vacuum will produce false rumors and could ultimately hurt morale. Sharing financial information shows employees the direct financial result of their collective efforts. However, this does not mean that you should directly email the financial statements from your accountant to all employees. Instead, here are some suggested alternatives:

- *Explain how the company makes money and where it goes.* I once did this in one of my rapidly growing companies with a 100 $1 bills. Using these dollar bills, I demonstrated to all the employees where the money goes when we receive an order for $100. For example, $50 went to pay for the cost of the product, $20 went to pay employees, $5 for the rent, etc. At the end, I showed how we were left with $10 out of every $100.

- *Share just enough.* Use a subset of the profit and loss statement to show overall revenue, cost of goods, and major expense categories. Do not break down specific employee or department salaries. That way, no one person can be easily identified. Show a comparison to past performance and future goals. Owners should share balance sheet and cash flow information when they want to highlight financial strengths or a growing weakness. Share information in a format that nonfinancial people can understand like bar charts and percentages. Remember, though, that most employees are familiar with a checkbook, bank account, and family budgets.

- *Stress the confidential nature of this information.* These numbers should never get out to competitors. However, general financial performance is a lot less valuable to competitors than other confidential information that employees have access to. For example, customer lists, product specifications, and processes.

- *Be transparent.* Companies should operate on the assumption that there are very few secrets in an Internet-connected world.

And where cameras are on every device. Confidential information from a small business is not difficult to access by competitors. Valued employees also expect transparency and honesty from you in order to build a supportive culture. However, it is also acceptable to say "no" when you believe disclosing something will hurt the business.

- *Get insights.* A benefit of this approach is that employees will offer a different point of view. They will know how each of the departments is doing, and competition inside a company is usually a good thing. As a result, employees will feel part of the solution, rather than simply a company expense. This exercise can bring any concerns to the forefront instead of having them fester in the background.

Be patient because this process takes a long time. Start by disclosing small amounts of financial information and increase it as employees absorb the implications of this data.

Fire the accountant who isn't working for you. Unfortunately, many owners see their accountant as the enemy and don't use them as part of their company. If this is the case, it's time to let your accountant go and bring in someone new who can really help. Here are the symptoms:

- *They don't explain the financial statements in a way you can understand.* You don't understand your own financial statements because you never learned how to read them. Unfortunately, some accountants don't help. They would rather keep the owner uneducated on this subject as some type of weird power over them. If this is the case, find an accountant who will explain the financial statements to your level of understanding. They should also teach you how to use the reports in your accounting program so you can get information and analyze it independently.

- *They don't know a specific industry.* Do they know your business? While many companies are alike, always get references from their clients that are in similar industries before hiring them.

- *They don't help maximize deductions.* When you sign your tax return, you are ultimately responsible for the treatment of deductions for your business. Some accountants are too lenient while others are too strict. Get enough information from the accountant to make an educated decision. You can also ask others in similar industries if they take advantage of specific deductions.

- *You can get better advice elsewhere.* If you find that you get better advice from asking other people or you read an article that you should have heard about from your accountant, it's time to start looking for a new one. If you are bringing more suggestions to your accountant than they are bringing to you, it's time to move on.

- *You are afraid to call because they charge by the minute.* You need to look at the overall value you receive for your accounting expense. If you are worrying about the cost of every minute, you are not getting the value you deserve. In most small businesses under $5 million in sales, accounting expenses should not exceed $10,000 a year.

- *They don't return phone calls in a timely fashion.* Their customer service stinks or they can't get paperwork filed in a timely manner. This should not be the case, even during tax season! This is a huge red flag.

CASE STUDY
HOW I LOST $1 MILLION
SCITECH

In the 1980s, I graduated with a business degree from Northwestern University—and I couldn't read a financial statement. This didn't seem important until I was running my own companies in the 1990s. I made all the mistakes that I described in this section. Most important, I didn't check my financial statements regularly, and I certainly wasn't in any position to use them to run my company.

In 1999, when I eventually sold the company, I lost one million dollars on the sale price because I couldn't read a balance sheet. I didn't understand what every number meant and why certain negative figures should have been positive. This reduced the value of the company when assessed by the buyer. Lesson learned. Before I started my next business in the following year, I learned how to read every number on financial statements!

CHAPTER 24

You Think Business Is About Growing Sales

WHY YOU ARE STUCK

You think business success is about revenue. You are so focused on the top sales line; you forget to check how much cash you have in the bank. In fact, you have outsourced most of the financial knowledge in your company and you accept what they tell you.

You are growing yourself broke. You are so busy bragging about how fast your company is growing and how many employees you are adding, that you don't have enough cash to fund it all. You are constantly in a cash crunch as you face shortages with payroll and pay other routine bills. You are unable to borrow more money from the bank to alleviate the pressure. Your monthly expenses typically exceed your sales. Your prices are too low, or your company routinely offers too many discounts. There is overhead in the company that does not contribute to the bottom line. You pay your bills early, and it takes too long to collect accounts receivable.

You can't read a cash flow statement. You never learned and are afraid to ask your accountant. No one balances the checking accounts in your business, so you have no idea how much cash you have now or will have at the end of the month.

HOW TO GET UNSTUCK

It's cash flow, stupid. It was reported in the 1992 presidential election that James Carville, Bill Clinton's campaign manager, had a sign posted in their Little Rock office that simply stated: "It's the economy, stupid." This was a reminder to everyone who worked at the campaign that the only thing the national race was about was the economy. The campaign should always focus on this one point.

That year, I started my third business after failing in two others. This time, I made my own sign and tacked it up in my office so it read: "It's cash flow, stupid." It became my daily reminder and mantra. Starting out in my first business in the 1980s, I thought the only thing that mattered was to sell my product to whoever would buy it. I reasoned that if you make sales, you eventually make money. This worked great until customers didn't pay me on time or at the same rate as my business expenses grew. Unfortunately, even if my customers did not pay their bills when they were due, my employees and vendors still wanted to be paid on time. My employees were not very interested in taking my accounts receivables in trade for their salaries or promises that I would pay them in a few weeks. What I realized is that sales do not pay bills. What your profit and loss statement says about profits in your small business can be meaningless. The news is filled with public companies that "misstate" their profit and loss statements and balance sheets to make their companies seem profitable. Only collecting the cash from sales in a business means something.

Cash is the gasoline that makes your business engine run. Without cash, your business suffocates. Cash is not only king, but also it is every other winning card in the deck. Most businesses fail because they run out of cash leaked through losses or other poor management practices.

Sales is vanity, cash flow is sanity. There are many things to do to improve your cash flow in your own business. First, open your monthly bank statement to check if you have more or less cash when comparing the beginning month to the end-of-month balance. Next, have your accountant construct a monthly cash flow statement for you. Most basic accounting software packages have a standard report that will produce it in some form. Learn what every positive and negative number on the statement means. Unfortunately, like me, most business owners use this tool only after they run into cash flow problems. In financial terms, cash flow is defined as cash receipts minus cash payments received over a given period of time. It's really the flow of money in and out of your business. Essentially, the rate of cash inflows and outflows determine your business's health. This is why a bank statement is the first place to start.

Learn to read the cash flow statement. Don't outsource the math. How much positive operating cash flow does your business produce? Profit is important, but cash flow is king. This number is found in your business cash flow statements. By definition, cash flow is your monthly profit, plus the change in accounts payable, the change in accounts receivable, and the change in inventory. The higher this number is monthly, the healthier your company is.

Here is what is typically on the cash flow statement:

- *Net income:* This is from the profit and loss statement discussed in Chapter 23.

- *Change in accounts receivable:* If this goes down, then the number is positive and it is a source of cash. In other words, your company is collecting its money faster. If this number goes up, then this number is negative and it is a use of cash.

- *Change in accounts payable.* If this goes down, then the number is negative and it is a use of cash. If this number goes up, then this number is positive and it is a source of cash. A positive number means your company is able to pay its bills later.

- *Change in accounts receivable:* If this goes down, then it is a source of cash, meaning less money is tied up in inventory and it's typically turning faster. If this number goes up, then it is a use of cash (or more money tied up in inventory).

- *Other categories can include loans from banks or other sources:* If the number goes up, then your company has borrowed more money, so this is a source of cash. If the number goes down, you company has paid down its loans, so this is a use of cash.

Turn the knobs to make more cash. Collecting your receivables faster or being extended credit from your vendors will boost your cash. Selling inventory faster and keeping your inventory levels lower will also accomplish the same thing. Buying inventory, only to have it sit for months on your shelf waiting for customer orders can take a lot of cash out of the business. Other ideas to bring more cash into your business include getting your customers to pay with credit cards. This way, you get money you can use in your checking account the next day. Give customers discounts for paying their bills sooner. With interest rates low, you may offer a half-percent discount for paying within ten days. Ask customers to pay a deposit or an advance for services before you perform it. This is industry practice in consulting companies.

Set a collection goal. The Days Sales Outstanding (DSO) for your business should never be more than 133% of your invoice terms. For example, if your company's terms are thirty days, all money should be collected within forty days of the invoice. Remember, reducing the collection of money from forty-five days to thirty days will save the company two weeks of cash. For a company that sells $100,000 a month, this could be an extra $50,000 of cash for you to put into your pocket or use for company expansion.

If practical, bill your customers as soon as you perform the service or deliver the product. Don't wait until the end of the month to send them a statement. Don't assume that a customer has thirty days to pay. Post on the invoice that payment is due "upon receipt." Be diligent about collecting your accounts receivables. State a specific date the payment is due. Call soon after the bill is sent out to make sure they received it and ask when it will be paid. Follow up early and often. The week before an invoice is scheduled to be paid, call to see if it is in the check run. If the check is not received, call again. Most companies want to pay their bills on time, and the inquiring vendor always gets paid first. In addition, you have a right to be paid within terms, so don't be timid about asking for your money.

Finally, remember a real customer pays their bill in the agreed time-frame. Don't extend credit to a customer that has not proven they can pay in a timely fashion. Never forget that credit is a privilege, not a right.

Remember, the business transaction isn't complete until the check clears the bank. In the long run, it only makes business sense to sell something to a customer you know will pay you. Doing work for a customer where you question if you'll ever be paid is not a sustainable business model. It is much better to have no work at all and, instead, spend your time finding real paying customers.

Earn later payments. Alternately, try to get 60-day or 90-day terms in which to pay your bills. If your vendors allow it, pay your own bills with credit cards after thirty days. This gives you thirty more days to pay until your credit card bill comes due. Track your inventory carefully. Know what sells quickly and what never moves off the shelf. Know how long your customer will wait for a product and still be satisfied. This will determine the setting of reorder points (when a product is reordered to be put into inventory) and the reorder quantities (how much is reordered).

Keep employees variable and available. Underused resources are a waste and a real drag on the bottom line. This happens in many companies with their employees who don't work at their maximum potential because the pace of the business alternates between very busy and extremely slow. Try to pay these resources only when they work. This can be done by using freelancers or other outsourcing resources.

Pay less rent. Unless you run a retail store, look to lower the cost of your rent. Many companies do not need a big central space for all employees to work. Technology has enabled most companies to collaborate effectively over the web. Think about how you can replace the rent expense with becoming a virtual company or by sharing space.

Lower employee turnover. Many employees stay at a company two years or less. That's a 50% turnover rate! This is very expensive since it costs 20% of an employee's salary to replace them.[20] In high turnover, low-paying jobs, this figure tends to be a slightly lower 16%, but the costs add up as quickly as employees walk out the door. Not all costs can be measured in dollars. Having a high turnover rate can prevent existing employees from making loyal connections with each other. This lack of a committed culture decreases the productivity inside every company. In addition, if you need to hire quickly, you run the risk of rushing the decision and making a bad hire. This could drop the productivity of the position, or even require you to fire that employee and hire all over again.

CASE STUDY
IT'S CASH FLOW, STUPID
SCITECH

In my last company, cash flow was a challenge. I had to buy inventory and pay for it before the products were sold. Many customers were large corporations or government agencies that paid net 60-days. We also had to invest in printing a mail order catalog and sending it to prospects far in advance of them buying a single product. Many vendors were small companies or individuals that insisted on being paid when their product was sent to us. This produced a huge cash flow strain.

To maximize cash, I implemented these steps:

- No matter how big they were, no credit was given to businesses or government agencies that did not have a buying history. Many individuals inside these organizations actually had credit cards they could use for purchases under $1,000.

- Credit terms were given for thirty days, and strict systematic collection tactics were used as described in this chapter.

- Net 60-day terms were fine for all vendors, as long as we were going to stock their product. If not, those products were drop-shipped to the customer.

- An in-stock fill rate of 90% was instituted, with reorder points set low (ten days' supply) and reorder quantities set low (ten days' supply).

- A target-inventory turn rate was set at twenty-four times a year.

CHAPTER 25

Your Fixed Overhead Costs Are Too High

WHY YOU ARE STUCK

Your sales and expense forecasts are off. You are too optimistic on both the increase in sales and the company's ability to control its expenses. You consistently think that sales will be higher next month or next quarter. You also are not able to track your true expenses, and the final number on your financial statements always surprises you. While your fixed expenses may be a bit high, you keep talking about "economies of scale" when your sales ramp up. You are confident this is when the real profit will role in.

You let your ego control the checkbook. You hire people, rent a fancy space, and go on trips you can't afford that have no direct return for your business. You make long-term financial commitments without having the revenue to back them up. You are so concerned about appearing to be successful that you have forgotten the path to actually making money. You think back on the excesses wasted during the go-go days of the 1999 Internet bubble and wonder if you are making the same mistakes.

You don't know the difference between a fixed and variable cost. You think all costs are the same and don't separate the two out on your financial statements. You only see costs growing, and you are not sure how to control them. You are thinking a 10% across-the-board cut might work.

You don't know the true costs of all your employees. You think it's just their salary, but you have forgotten about all the other costs of employment, including turnover. This is one of the reasons why you can never seem to make a profit.

HOW TO GET UNSTUCK

Practice the art of forecasting. Predicting sales and expenses takes experience and practice. A good place to start is to look at past company performance. In the future, what factors internally and externally are changing that will affect both sales and expenses? When in doubt, cut forecasted revenue by 50% and double expected expenses. Identify what factors will actually affect sales because many cause-and-effect relationships simply are not true. For many small business owners, expenses are easier to track, but their increase does not necessarily lead to more revenue. Budget before the beginning of each new year and track progress on a monthly basis. Make changes if the budget is severely missed on a quarterly basis.

Factor in all employee costs, not just their salary. The largest fixed cost in most small businesses is employees. A worker's salary is just the first of many employee-related costs. Here's how much you should estimate to add on top of salary to calculate the total cost per employee:

- *Employer share of payroll taxes:* Add 11%, which includes state and federal unemployment taxes, Medicare, and Social Security FICA (6.2%). These costs typically need to be paid monthly to various government agencies.

- *Paid time off:* Add 1% for vacation, holidays, sick time, and jury duty. Most employees will take off twenty days per year.

- *Health insurance:* Add 5%. It has become traditional now for the employer to split the cost fifty-fifty. Increase this cost if you plan to pay the entire premium or include the employee's family. Some companies add life and disability insurance.

- *401(k):* Many employers match up to 6% of the employee contribution.

- *Other perks:* Add 3%. This could be holiday bonuses, health club membership, public commuter passes, or tuition reimbursements.

- *Managing or outsourcing the payroll and HR function:* Add 1%.

- *Work tools:* Add 4%. This includes computers, smartphones, tablets, and supplies.

- *Employee training:* New employees need time to acclimate to the corporate processes and culture. There is a cost for time when they are not being productive in their job. This can take up to three months, depending on the position.

Understand what true employee utilization is. Key in building a profitable service-based business is to understand how billable an employee needs to be. For a company to have a 50% gross profit margin, employees need to be billable at least 85% of the time. For example, there are 2,080 work hours in a year. If an employee takes four weeks off for vacation and holidays, this leaves 1,920 billable hours. If an employee is 85% utilized, then they bill 1,632 hours a year. Underutilization of billable employees is the key reason why service businesses have low gross margins. Many times, multiple employees are billing 2,000 hours a year. In addition, an employee must bill at three times their salary cost.

The math looks like this:

- If an employee costs $30 an hour, there may be additional costs with taxes and benefits of 30% x $30 = $10.

- The total employee cost then would be $40 an hour x 2,080 hours per year for $83,200 per year.

- If the employee is billed to customers at an hourly rate of $90, their total revenue billed per year will be $90 x 1,920 = $172,800.

- On this revenue, the gross margin is $172,800 - $83,200 = $89,600 (52%).

These metrics will build a profitable company.

Increase your number of revenue-generating employees. A small business owner needs to categorize their employees as overhead or revenue generating. Few employees should be categorized as expenses. The goal is to have as many revenue-generating employees as possible. It is also important to keep as many of the costs variable (as it relates to revenue), for all employees, and at the same time available for the company to be able to use them when needed. While this is a difficult balance, it ensures that expenses are only incurred when there are sales.

Understand which fixed costs are essential. The key to success in any economy is to keep fixed costs as low as possible. This is commonly referred to as the company's overhead. It's the costs to run your business that do not vary based on the level of revenue. This means that whether your company is selling one or a thousand products this month, the fixed cost will be the same. While fixed overhead may be masked when your business is growing, it will cause cash flow issues when your company sales are shrinking. Keeping all fixed costs to a bare minimum better positions small business owners to manage their downside risk. You may think that some traditional expenses are fixed, but many times, they can be cut or eliminated. This type of analysis will determine if you are investing for the future, or if the costs are just assumed overhead added over time and serves no productive purpose. Question all expense assumptions annually.

Rent is a good example. Many small business owners get trapped by their landlords. During the start-up or high-growth phase of any company, the owner tends to lease more space than they need. They are caught in the fantasy of large offices and do big build-outs. Landlords know what to feed an entrepreneur: their ego!

Unfortunately, when a business stops growing or shrinks, the large rent expense looms large on the profit and loss statement. Since many business owners are required to personally guarantee their lease, they lose the flexibility to move to a smaller space when their business goes sideways. This has been especially true during the Great Recession where many companies were paying rental rates far above current market rates or their space was too large for their shrinking company.

Before renting, think about whether this expense is a marketing or overhead expense. It is a marketing expense if the business is a retail store where location matters. In the vast majority of other nonretail businesses, a lot less location and size is actually needed. In fact, many small businesses now use the tools of technology to work together virtually. Great teamwork can be built using various online collaboration and video conferencing tools without incurring the expense of an office. This can also eliminate expenses like electricity, gas, renter's insurance, office supplies, repairs, maintenance, water, and parking. Reduction or elimination of these types of expenses can add upwards of 15% to the bottom line.

Trapped with a high rent? Ask the landlord for a reduction. Show them the company's dire financial statements. Remember, a company should be in business to make a profit for the owner, not just the landlord. Many owners are surprised how accommodating some landlords can be, especially if they are not able to rent the space to anyone else at the same price. Another strategy is to extend the lease with less space at a lower price.

Keep costs variable. Variable costs are only incurred with every new product or service sold. They are totally a function of sales. For example, inventory as a cost is variable and only incurred when a product is sold. Only keep very highly utilized employees or use freelancers and contractors for your workforce. Here are some ways to keep normally fixed expenses variable:

- **Advertising:** As discussed in previous chapters, any advertising should be traceable and trackable. This makes advertising much more of a variable cost, than a large fixed one. Test small amounts first and only scale when you find the relationship between advertising and sales. Supplement costly efforts with PR and social media.

- **Marketing and sales:** Getting customers is about creating long-term relationships with prospects and connectors (the people that are never buyers but can connect you to a buyer). This means staying in contact with them so they will think of your product when they or someone they know is ready to buy. Free email that provides something of value is an effective way to keep in contact with prospects monthly. Both Constant Contact and Vertical Response offer free entry-level solutions. Use a customer relationship management system (CRM) to track your phone or email conversations. Highrise by 37signals (makers of Basecamp) integrates with your email and is free for up to 250 contacts. Survey your customers to understand exactly the solutions they need by using SurveyMonkey. In social media, track what customers and competitors are saying about your company using free applications like Google Alerts, HootSuite, or TweetDeck. For your company website, WordPress has free downloadable themes. Surprisingly, there are many free hosting options for your website as well, although this may not be the best match for your company. To keep this department a variable expense, pay sales commission only or pay only based on hours with or calling customers. For marketing, hire a firm or a part-time employee for a limited time per week. Increase or decrease based on trailing six-month sales.

- **Human resources:** Outsource by the hour for particular advice or production of an HR manual and related documents.

- **Product development:** Outsource for a fixed-price contract and on-time delivery.

- **Interns:** Free or low-cost interns can be located at local universities. Hidden costs are management time and performance reviews so they can get college credit.

- **Finances:** Keeping track of your finances no longer needs to be done with a fancy accounting solution, especially if your business does not have inventory. Make bookkeeping easy using free tools like Mint or FreshBooks. More important, these solutions will even get your money collected faster by sending invoice notices electronically.

While many free or low-cost solutions may not be robust enough for your growing company, it demonstrates how to keep monthly fixed costs to a minimum and only scale them as needed. This does not mean that a company should not invest in overhead infrastructure. It means that every company should only invest as far ahead of the sales growth curve as makes sense for their industry. Always ask, "Do you really need to spend that now?" You would never build a fancy house if your family wasn't going to live in it, right? Do the same thing with your company.

CASE STUDY
SAVED VIRTUALLY
MRAJG MARKETING*

For ten years, MRAJG felt they needed a Madison Avenue address to compete with other New York marketing firms. They serviced Fortune 500 clients and wanted to project this professional image.

A few years back, their rent and associated costs started to get very high, so they hired employees outside of the metropolitan area to prevent office expansion. They installed companywide collaboration tools so the people who worked remotely could work with those inside the office. Three years ago, this was so successful the company decided to do away with the rented office and have all employees work from home. This has saved them over $150,000 a year.

Fictional company

AFTERWORD

Now What?

If you're reading this book, there are likely many ways you think your business is stuck. You are not alone. Not all these problems crept up overnight and they will not all be solved in a single day or with one magic formula. It is key to strive for "minimal achievement." Most of us try to accomplish too many things at the same time, and in the end, achieve very little.

Instead, pick one of the 25 reasons in this book to focus on first. Do not go onto the second until that one changes to your satisfaction.

Be patient with yourself. Running a small business is not a race, but a way to live a passionate, enjoyable, and financially successful life.

I will always be here to help, and I would love to hear from you.

E-mail: Barry@Moltz.com

Website: www.barrymoltz.com

On Facebook, Twitter, LinkedIn, Pinterest and Google Plus:

Barry Moltz

ENDNOTES

1. "Total Number of iPods Sold All-Time." About.com. http://ipod.about.com/od/glossary/qt/number-of-ipods-sold.htm.

2. "12 Reasons to Stop Multitasking Now"- FoxNews.com. www.foxnews.com/health/2013/06/18/12-reasons-to-stop-multitasking-now/

3. "12 Reasons to Stop Multitasking Now"- FoxNews.com. www.foxnews.com/health/2013/06/18/12-reasons-to-stop-multitasking-now/

4. "How often do you check your phone? The average person does it 110 times a DAY (and up to every 6 seconds in the evening)" DailyMail.com. www.dailymail.co.uk/sciencetech/article-2449632/How-check-phone-The-average-person-does-110-times-DAY-6-seconds-evening.html

5. "80% of Americans work an extra 30 hours a month on their own time" Digital Journal.com. www.digitaljournal.com/article/327825

6. "Fourth and Go For It " SportsonEarth.com. www.sportsonearth.com/article/62665328

7. "Startup Business Failure Rate By Industry" StatisticBrain.com. www.statisticbrain.com/startup-failure-by-industry/

8. Urban Dictionary. /www.urbandictionary.com/define.php?term=Syfy

9. "Where Does It Hurt?" Sandler Training. www.corporatestrategies.sandler.com/pressitems/show/2536/213

10. "Apple Ad Budget Hits $1 Billion" CBSNews.com. www.cbsnews.com/news/apples-ad-budget-hits-1-billion/

11. "Learn from the 7 business models that failed in 2011" BoardofInnovation.com. www.boardofinnovation.com/2012/01/19/learn-from-the-7-business-models-that-failed-in-2011/

12. "Alaska Air, JetBlue top airline satisfaction ratings" USAToday.com. www.usatoday.com/story/todayinthesky/2013/05/15/alaska-air-jetblue-top-airline-satisfaction-ratings/2161535/

13. "Forget About That Cash Bonus" Harvard Business Review. http://blogs.hbr.org/2013/03/forget-about-that-cash-bonus/

14. "Forget About That Cash Bonus" Harvard Business Review. http://blogs.hbr.org/2013/03/forget-about-that-cash-bonus/

15. "Ego" Comicvine.com. www.comicvine.com/ego/4005-19936/

16. "Do Bosses Have to Be Cutthroat" NYTimes.com. http://boss.blogs.nytimes.com/2012/03/28/do-good-bosses-have-to-have-to-be-cut-throat/?_r=0

17. "The Secret to Same Day Delivery: When Overnight Isn't Fast Enough" OpenForum.com. /www.openforum.com/articles/when-overnight-delivery-isnt-fast-enough/

18. "Smartphones Should Know Their Place at Work" NYTimes.com. www.nytimes.com/2012/03/11/jobs/etiquette-for-using-personal-technology-at-work-career-couch.html?_r=0If

19. "A Journalist's Guide to Reading Financial Statements" MediaBistro.com. www.mediabistro.com/10000words/how-to-read-financial-statements-for-journalists_b24602

20. "How Much Does It Cost to Lose Employees" CBSNews.com. www.cbsnews.com/news/how-much-does-it-cost-companies-to-lose-employees/